COINS
OF
MEDIAEVAL INDIA

FROM
THE SEVENTH CENTURY
DOWN TO
THE MUHAMMADAN CONQUESTS

COINS
OF
MEDIAEVAL INDIA

FROM

THE SEVENTH CENTURY
DOWN TO
THE MUHAMMADAN CONQUESTS

BY

MAJOR-GENERAL SIR A. Cunningham

K.C.I.E., C.S.I., R.E.

GYAN

Published by

GYAN

Gyan Publishing House
5, Ansari Road
Daryaganj, New Delhi-110002
Phone: 011-47034999, 9811692060
E-mail: books@gyanbooks.com

Distribution Network
gyanbooks.com
India, USA, Canada, UK, Australia, France

ISBN : 978-81-212-2710-0 (HB)
First Published, 1894

2nd Impression 2021

Printed at: Gyan Press, Delhi.

Coins of Mediaeval India
Author: A. Cunningham

COINS

OF

MEDIÆVAL INDIA

FROM

THE SEVENTH CENTURY

DOWN TO

THE MUHAMMADAN CONQUESTS

BY

MAJOR-GENERAL SIR A. CUNNINGHAM

K.C.I.E., C.S.I., R.E.

LONDON

B. QUARITCH, 15, PICCADILLY

1894

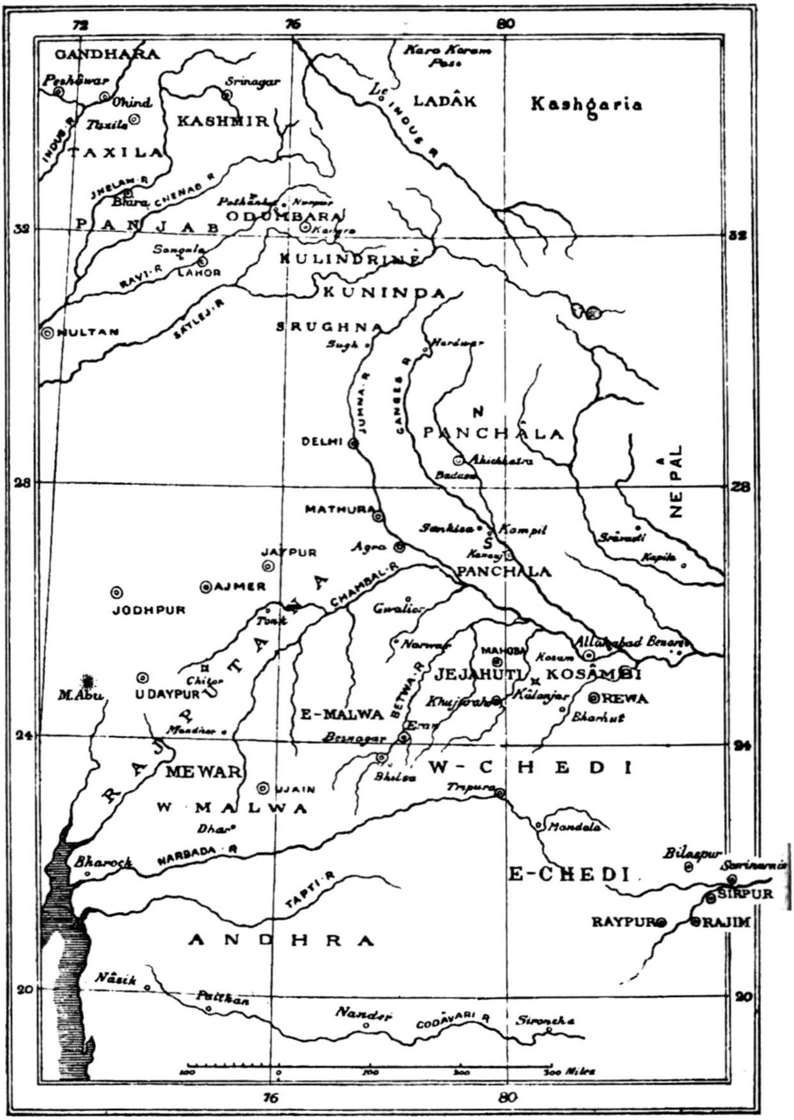

PANJAB AND N-W-INDIA.

PREFACE.

THE successful irruption of the White Huns into Northern India in the beginning of the sixth century A.D. gave the first shock to the stability of the great Gupta Empire, which had lasted for two centuries without a check. The western provinces of Malwa and Rajputâna, from the Narbada to the Jumna as far east as Gwalior, were seized and held by the conquerors, while the Gangetic provinces were overrun and plundered and the temples destroyed as far east as Magadha. From that time the eastern provinces were in an unsettled and disturbed state, and the power of the Guptas began rapidly to decline. Most of the states whose coins are described in the following pages rose to power and established their independence during the following two centuries.

The coinage which under the Guptas had been continued on a settled system of *dinars* of gold, and *half kârshas* of silver, began very early to be debased. In the western provinces the old thick *drammas* of silver were given up for small thin pieces copied from the Sassanian money, but without any letters or legends to show by whom they were issued. The Indo-Scythian type of the copper money was continued in the Panjab and Kashmir down to the beginning of the fourteenth century. The coin types of the Horseman and Bull of the Brahmans of Kabul were continued by the Ghaznavis, by the Ghoris, and by the different Rajput states of the North-West of India. And lastly, the Indian type of the Goddess Parvati, introduced by the Rajas of Chedi, was adopted by the Chandellas of Mahoba, by the Tomaras of Delhi, by the Rahtors of Kanauj, and even by Muhammad bin Sâm. All these different types are described in the following pages.

A. C.

[The author of this work died on 28th November, 1893, whilst it was passing through the press. The author's sons are indebted to Mr. E. J. Rapson, of the British Museum, for kindly reading and correcting the whole of the proofs.]

COINS OF MEDIÆVAL INDIA.

Unpublished Coins of Ancient India.

In my account of the *Coins of Ancient India*, I purposely omitted the coins of the Western Satraps of Malwa and Surâshtra, as well as the coins of the Guptas of Magadha, because both series had already been very fully described; the former by Pandit Bhagwân Lâl, in the *Royal Asiatic Society Journal*, and the latter by Mr. Vincent Smith in the same journal. But since these papers were published some new coins have been obtained, and as some of them are of considerable interest, I think it is right to make them known at once.

Plate I., Fig. 1.—Copper coin of Taxila; 0·7 inch, 61 grains—a very perfect coin.

Obv.—*A Bodhi Tree* surrounded by Buddhist railing—*Swastika* and *Taurine* in field.

Rev.—The *Taxila symbol* in a circle. (See *Coins of Ancient India*, Pl. II.)

Plate I., Fig. 2.—Copper coin of Râjputâna: 0·7 inch, 121 grains; in fine preservation.

Obv.—*Humped Bull*, standing to left, surrounded by a radiated circle.

Rev.—*Male figure* with right hand raised. Indian legend, *Râjna Janapadasa.* (See *Coins of Ancient India*. Pl. VIII., Fig. 19.)

I take this opportunity to describe some other ancient coins, which are not given in the Plate.

No. 3.—Square copper coin, 56 grains, with Indian monogram forming *Yajnabhu* quite clearly.

No. 4.—Round copper coin, 82 grains.

Obv.—Standing female.

Rev.—Bodhi tree, with Indian legend, *Agedake-Abhi cha ja.* The capital A's are both initial letters.

No. 5.—Round copper coin, 120 grains.

Obv.—Humped bull walking to right.

Rev.—Bodhi tree. Indian legend, *Abhi cha Mitasa.*

No. 6.—Round white metal coin, 36 grains.

Obv.—Lion with tail curled over back. Indian legend, five letters, *S* only being distinct.

No. 7.—Duplicate, 52 grains. Legend lost.

No. 8.—Round copper coin, 99 grains.

Obv.—Elephant.

Rev.—Female standing. Indian legend overhead . . *Bhagavata.*

I.—Western Satraps.

The long series of silver coins found in Mâlwa, Gujarat, and the adjacent provinces, which have been described by Prinsep, Thomas, and others, under the name of the "Sah Kings of Surâshtra," are now known as the "Coins of the Western Satraps." The title, first read as "*Sah,*" as we now know from well-preserved coins and inscriptions, is properly either *Sinha* or *Sena.* The mistake originated in the small letters of the coin legends which were generally wanting in vowels. The series has been very fully described by the late Pandit Bhagwân Lâl Indraji, and carefully edited and illustrated by Mr. E. J. Rapson, of the British Museum.[1]

The coins of the Western Satraps begin with *Nahapâna,* whose inscriptions are dated in the years 41 and 46, which I would tentatively assign to the era of the Mâlwas, beginning in B.C. 57. I am led to this assignment by the fact that some of his coins were certainly found at Ajmer in Rajputâna, while his conquests to the south would seem to be due to his son-in-law *Ushânadatta,* a Saka chief. Two of his coins, obtained at Ajmer, I now give in Plate I., Figs. 4 and 5.

The family of Nahapâna was succeeded by *Chashtana,* the Tiastanes of Ptolemy, whose capital was Ujain. His date is now, I believe, accepted as beginning with the Saka era in A.D. 79. Of himself and some of his successors I give a few coins in Plate I., to supplement the Pandit's account.

The silver coins of these Satraps are evident copies of the Greek hemidrachms, of which, as we know from the Periplus, those of Menander and Apollodotus were still current at Barygaza as late as the latter end of the first century A.D. They are apparently copies of the Philopator coins of Apollodotus.

The copper coins of these Satraps are of purely Indian origin. The Bodhi-tree, and the Dharma Chakra Pillar, are both common types of the early Buddhist coins. The humped bull, the elephant, and the chaitya are also well-known Buddhist types. But the thunderbolt and the arrow, which appear on all the known coins of Nahapâna, are quite new types.

The coins of Rudra Sinha, son of Satya Sinha, No. 13,

---

[1] *Journal Royal Asiatic Society*, vol. xxii., p. 639.

and of Sinha Sena, the sister's son of Rudra Sinha, No. 14, are both dated, the former in Varshe 310, and the latter in Varshe 304. My last addition is a coin of Rudra Sinha, No. 15, on which he takes the title of Maharaja Kshatrapa.

Pandit Bhagwân Lâl has drawn attention to the fact that *Sak. Sam.* 171 = A.D. 249, the latest date of Vijaya Sena, is the initial point of the *Trikutika Era*; and I may add also of the Chedi Era.

WESTERN SATRAPS.

A.D.	No.	S.S. on coins.	A.D. on coins.		Other dates.
79	I.	—	—	CHASHTANA	
110	II.	—	—	Jayadâman	
130	III.	72	150	Rudra Dâman	
170	IV.	—	—	Dâmajâda Sri	
175	V.	100	178	Jivadâman	
180	VI.	103	181	Rudra Sinha	118
200	VII.	122	200	Rudra Sena	125-142
222	VIII.	144	222	Sanghadâman	
222	IX.	144	222	Prithivi Sena	
225	X.	148	226	Dâma Sena	157
232	XI.	154	232	Dâmajada Sri	
236	XII.	158	236	Viradâman	
238	XIII.	160	238	Yasodâman	161
238	XIV.	160	238	Vijaya Sena	171 = A.D. 249
255	—	—	—	ISWARA-DATTA	
258	XV.	180	258	Dâmajada Sri	190
258	XVI.	180	258	Rudra Sena	188
278	XVII.	200	278	Bhartridâman	214
276	XVIII.	198	276	Viswa Sinha	203
—	XIX.	?	—	Sinha Sena	
290	XX.	216	294	Viswa Sena	223
—	XXI.	—	—	JIVA-DÂMAN	No coins
305	XXII.	231	309	Rudra Sinha	240
315	XXIII.	240	318	Yasodâman	246
—	XXIV.	—	—	RUDRA-DÂMAN	No coins
345	XXV.	270	348	Rudra Sena	295
—	XXVI.	—	—	SATYA SINHA	No coins
378	XXVII.	300	378	Rudra Sinha	
382	XXVIII.	304	382	Sinha Sena	

GENEALOGY OF WESTERN SATRAPS.

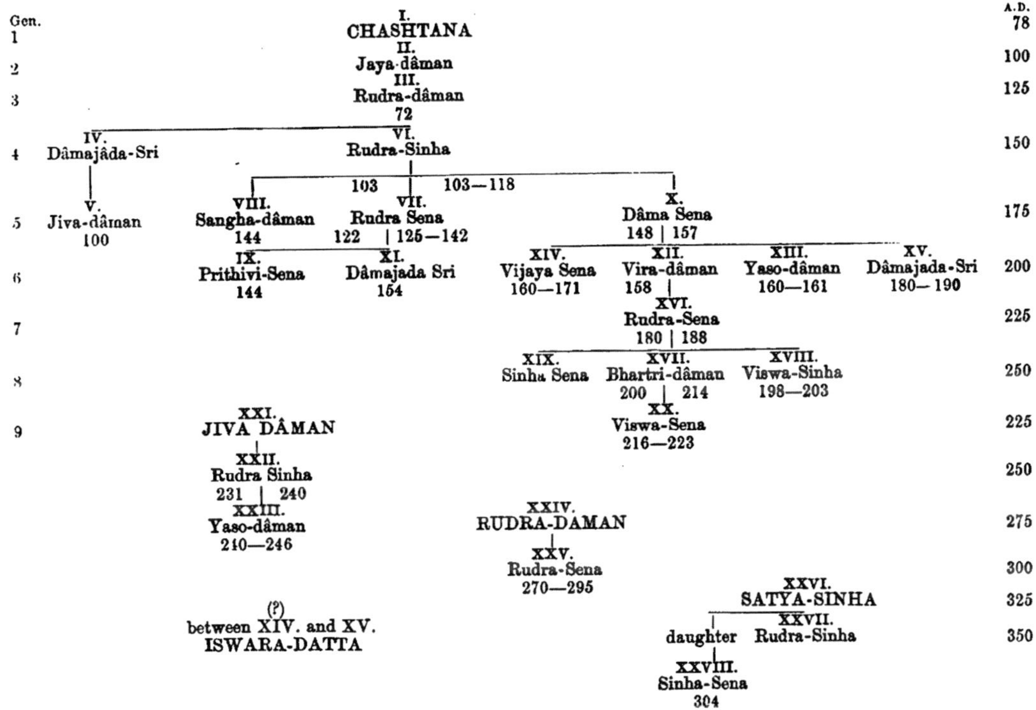

PLATE I. No.	Metal.	Grs.	
			NAHAPÂNA.
3	AR		British Museum, from Bhagwân Lâl, see his Plate, Fig. 1—Junagarh in Gujarât. *Head of King* to right. Remains of Greek legend to left, unread. *Arrow and Thunderbolt.* Indian legend, *Râjnah Kshaharâtasa Nahapânasa.* Gandharian legend, *Rânah Chhaharâtasa Nahapânasa.*[2]
4	Æ		Author, from Pushkar, near Ajmer. Bhagwân Lâl, Fig. 1*a*. *Arrow and Thunderbolt.* Indian legend not clear, but apparently *Nahapâna* . . *Deer and Dharma-chakra* on Pillar. Legend apparently Greek, . . ΙΛΕΩC .
5	Æ		Author, from Ajmer. *Arrow and Thunderbolt.* Indian legend distinct, *Nahapânasa.* *Bodhi Tree*, surrounded by Buddhist railin .
			CHASHTANA.
6	AR	25	Author, from Gujarât. *Head of King* to right, with collar round neck. Some Greek letters. *Chaitya.* Sun with 16 rays to right; crescent to left; snake or waved line below. Indian legend, *Rajno Mahakshatrapasa Ghsamotika putrasa Chashtanasa.* Gandharian legend, *Chathaṇasa.*
			JAYA-DÂMAN.
7	Æ	28	Author, from Pushkar, near Ajmer; square coin, see Bhagwân Lâl, Fig. 3*a*. *Indian Bull* to right; in front, trident and axe combined. Indian legend, *Jaya-dâman*, incomplete. *Four circles*, joined by a cross; the symbol of Ujain.

[2] This Gandharian legend (in *Kharoshtri* letters) was first pointed out by me.

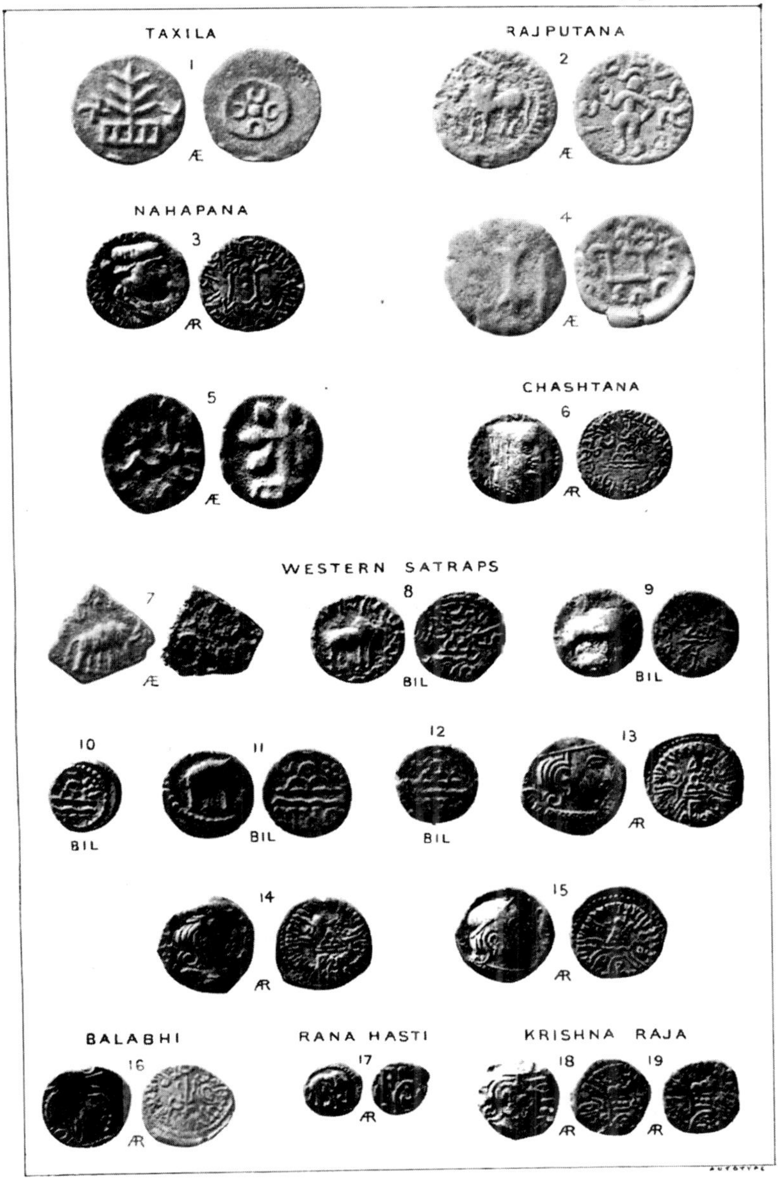

WESTERN SATRAPS OF MALWA AND GUJARAT.

PLATE I.

No.	Metal.	Grs.	
			JIVA-DAMAN.
8	Bil.	24	Author, from Pushkar, near Ajmer; unique; apparently Billon. *Humped Bull* to right; long inscription; Greek letters. *Chaitya*, with sun and moon; waved line below. Indian legend, *Rājnah mahakshatrapasa, Jiva-dāmasa.*
			RUDRA-DÂMAN.
9	Bil.	38	Author, from Pushkar, near Ajmer; unique; apparently Billon. *Humped Bull* to right. Legend illegible. *Chaitya*, with sun and moon; waved line below. Indian legend, *Rājnah Mahakshatrapasa Rudra Dāmasa.*
			ANONYMOUS COINS.
10	Bil.	21	Author, from Ujain and Sârangpur in Mâlwa. *Elephant* to right, surrounded by circle of dots. *Chaitya*, with sun and moon; waved line below. Date in Indian figures, 129 = Rudra-Sena.
11	Bil.	29	Author, from Ujain. Types as No. 10, with date of 147 = Dâma-Sena.
12	Bil.	20	Author, from Ujain. Types as No. 10, with date of 153 = Vira-Dâman.
			RUDRA-SINHA, son of SATYA-SINHA.
13	Æ	27	Author, from Pushkar, near Ajmer. *Head of Satrap* to right; date behind head, *Varshe*, 310 (?) *Chaitya*, with sun and moon. Indian legend, *Rājno Mahakshatrapasa Swāmi Satya Sinhasa putrasa.* *Rājno Mahakshatrapasa Swami Rudra Sinhasa.*

PLATE I.

No.	Metal	Grs.	
			SINHA-SENA.
14	Æ	28	Author, from Pushkar, near Ajmer. *Head of Satrap* to right; behind head, date *varshe*, 304. *Chaitya*, with sun and moon. Indian legend, *Rajno Mahákshatrapasa Swâmi Rudra Sinhasa.* *Rajno Mahâkshatrapasa Swasriyasa Swâmi Sinha Senasa.*
15	Æ	27	Author, from Pushkar, near Ajmer; unique. *Head of Satrap* to right. *Chaitya* with sun and moon. Indian legend, *Maharaja Kshatrapa Swâmi Rudra Sinha putrasa.* *Rano Mahakshatrapasa Swâmi Sinha Senasya.*
			BALABHI.
16	Æ	27	Author, from Pushkar, near Ajmer. *Head of King* to right. Trident. Indian legend, not read; tentative reading in Archæol. Survey, ix., 6, 29.
			RANA-HASTI.
17	Æ	7	Author, from Rajputana; rare. *Elephant* to right. *Rev.—Sri Raṇa Hasti*, in two lines.
			KRISHNA-RAJA RÂSHTRAKUTA.
18 19	Æ Æ		Author, from Râjputâna; *circa* A.D. 375—400. (See Archæol. Survey, vol. ix., 29. Pl. V., 26, 27, 28.) *Rude Head of King* with moustaches. No legend. *Recumbent Bull* to right. Indian legend, *Parama Maheswara Mahâditya Pâdânudhyâta, Sri Krishna Râja.*

II.—The Guptas of Magadha.

The genealogy of the Gupta family is derived from their inscriptions. The founder of the family was *Sri-Gupta*, towards the end of the third century, or about 260—270 A.D. He is mentioned under this name by one of the Chinese pilgrims, who visited India in A.D. 670, as the founder of a monastery for the reception of Chinese pilgrims, about five hundred years before his visit. As he only refers to the time as *about* five hundred years, we may accept his statement as only an approximation to the true period, or say somewhere about the third or fourth century A.D. Regarding this name, Mr. Vincent Smith has adopted Mr. Fleet's opinion that the *Sri* is only the usual honorific prefix of Rajas' names. This view I utterly reject, as it seems to me quite impossible that *Gupta* by itself could form a name. Like *Pàla, Datta, Dâsa, Rakshita*, it requires the addition of the name of some god or hero to form a name—without this addition it has no meaning. The Chinese pilgrims were aware of this, as they mention another *Sri-Gupta*, who tried to kill Buddha, with his full name of *She-li-kio-to*, or Sri-Gupta,[3] or "protected by Sri, *i.e.*, Lakshmi."

The date of the Guptas was for a long time doubtful, owing chiefly to a statement of Alberuni, which apparently meant that their era, the *Gupta-kâl*, was dated from their extinction. As they were lords paramount of North India for several centuries, the correct settlement of their date was very important. Luckily, their era is now fixed beyond all doubt, as starting from A.D. 319.

[3] I offer the English lawyer's name of *Ood-deen*, in his case of "Regina *v.* Ood-deen," as an equally absurd name for a Muhammadan.

The only difficulty was to ascertain whether the era began with *Sri Gupta* himself, who was only a simple *Mahâraja*, or with his grandson *Chandra Gupta I.*, who assumed the title of *Mahârâjâdhirâja*. I have always advocated the latter opinion, which is fully supported by the different dates which we possess of *Chandra Gupta II.*, *Kumâra Gupta*, and *Skanda Gupta*. Chandra Gupta II. dates in A.G. 83 and 92, or A.D. 401—410; Kumâra Gupta dates in A.G. 96 and 130, or A.D. 413 and 448; Skanda encountered the Hunas, probably under Toramâna, about 475. We thus have five generations from the accession of Chandra I. to Skanda's death in 160 years, or thirty-two years for each generation.

The genealogy from Sri Gupta to Skanda Gupta is derived from the Bhitari Pillar inscription; that from Sri Gupta to Kumâra Gupta II., from the Bhitari Seal. The former makes no mention of Puru Gupta, and the latter omits Skanda Gupta altogether. As each of them is stated to be a son of Kumâra Gupta I., the "troubles" at the end of the father's reign (Bhitari Pillar) were probably caused by the quarrels of the two sons for the succession. Skanda must have prevailed very soon after Kumâra's death, as we do not possess even a single coin of Puru Gupta, either in gold or in silver.

Dr. Hoërnle has suggested that the epithet of *pâdânudhyâta* applied to Puru Gupta, betokened his immediate succession to his father, but as the same epithet of "bowing to his father's feet" is applied to Skanda Gupta in the Bihar Pillar inscription, I conclude that each of these princes claimed to be the immediate successor of Kumâra Gupta. My impression is, that Skanda was the elder brother and rightful heir, and that the "troubles" which closed the reign of Kumâra Gupta (Bhitari Pillar inscription) were caused by the quarrels between the two brothers. Puru Gupta, as a young prince, may have been at court with his father, while Skanda may have been absent as viceroy of Mâlwa. We know certainly that Skanda Gupta prevailed after a short time, as we have his Junagarh inscription dating from A.G. 136, only a few years after Kumâra's latest coin dates. I would fix his succession to undisputed power in the Gupta year 134, or A.D. 152.

I take Budha Gupta to have been the son and successor to Skanda Gupta. His earliest date is A.G. 165, on the Eran Pillar, and his latest date, or 174 A.G., is on the silver coins which I got at Benares. The only coins yet found of Budha Gupta were the five specimens just mentioned, and a sixth found at Sârnath, near Benares. I would fix his reign from 162 to 180 of the Gupta era, or from A.D. 480 to 500. He was the last of the earlier Guptas who held rule over Mâlwa. A Bhânu Gupta is mentioned on a lingam pillar at Eran, in A.G. 191, or A.D. 509, but I believe that he was conquered by Toramâna, the leader of the White Huns.

After the death of Budha Gupta, the northern provinces were held by *Nara-sinha Gupta*, the son of Puru Gupta, and as he bears the title of Balâditya on his coins, I conclude, with some certainty, that he was the Balâditya of Magadha, who defeated *Mihirkul*, the son of Toramâna. He was undoubtedly a contemporary of that ruthless conqueror, and I would fix his date at from 182 to 212 of the Gupta era, or from A.D. 500 to 530. In Fig. 1 of Plate II. I have given one of these coins, which as long ago as 1854 I assigned to *Nara-Gupta Balâditya*. This reading Mr. Thomas described as "a very ancient myth" (*Jour. Bengal Asiatic Society*, xxiv. p. 386), and at a later date, in 1883, adopted it without acknowledgment. His reading of the coins of *Vishnu Gupta Chandrâditya,* in the same paper, was also adopted in the same manner from my list of coins in the India Office. The coin of Narasinha Gupta, in the present plate, shows the letter *Gu* between the king's feet very plainly. Mr. Vincent Smith reads *Gre,* which I have never met with.

The other Gupta gold coins in the Plate are introduced as novelties: No. 2, of Kumâra-Gupta II., Kramâditya, the son and successor of Nara Sinha Gupta; No. 3 is of Jaya Gupta; No. 4 is of Vishnu Gupta Chandrâditya; and No. 5 is of *Ṣaṣângka,* who persecuted the Buddhists, and closed the great temple of Mahâbodhi; with him the rule of the Guptas was closed for a time.

The copper coins of the Guptas are rare, especially the larger ones. Mr. Vincent Smith's paper gives the only full account of them. Since then I have received No. 6, which may perhaps belong to an earlier period, as the Bowl of Buddha standing in a Buddhist Railing cannot be assigned to the Guptas of Magadha. The name is [*Ha*]*ri Gupta.*

No. 8 is an undoubted Gupta coin of unusually large size, weighing 87 grains. The reverse has the Gupta standard symbol of *Garuda.*

I have placed a Gem Seal, No. 7, figured by H. H. Wilson in *Ariana Antiqua,* as an illustration of the Gupta copper coin. The name has been misread by Wilson as *Kusuma Dâsasya,* the "slave of the flower," instead of *Keṣava-dâsasya,* the "slave of Vishnu." The coins of Chandra Gupta I. show the king presenting a flower to his Queen Kumâra Devi. (See Mr. Rapson's No. 1 coin in *Num. Chron.*, Ser. III. vol. xi. Plate II.)

EARLIER GUPTAS.

A.D.	Gupta Era.		Gupta Era.	A.D.	Gupta Era.	
		Sri-Gupta . . .				
		Ghatotkacha . .				
		CHANDRA-GUPTA I.				
		Samudra Gupta . .				
		Chandra-Gupta II. .	82, 93			
		Kumâra-Gupta I. .	96, 98, 129, 130			
452	134	Skanda Gupta . .	136, 146, 149	450	132	Puru Gupta[4]
480	162	Budha Gupta . .	165, 174			
500	182	Bhânu Gupta . .	191	500	182	Narasinha-Gupta
509	191	TORAMÂNA . .		530	212	Kumâra Gupta II.
				550	232	Vishnu Gupta / Chandrâditya
				570	252	. . . .
				590	272	SASÂNGKA
				607	289	HARSHA-VARDHANA

[4] This name has been read as *Pura Gupta*, which is quite inadmissible. It is also read as *Sthira Gupta*, which is a synonym of *Skanda*.

In the Ain Akbari list of the kings of Malwa I find the names of—

Chandra-Pâl	=	Chandra Gupta II.
Mahendra Pâl	=	Kumâra Gupta I. Mahendra.
Karm Chand	=	Skanda Gupta, Kramâditya.

LATER GUPTAS AND MAUKHARIS.

A.D.	GUPTAS.	A.D.	MAUKHARIS.
500	Krishna Raja		Avanti Varma
520	Harsha Gupta		Aditya Varma
540	Jivita Gupta I.		Iswara Varma
560	Kumâra Gupta III.	560	Iṣâna Varma
580	Dâmodara Gupta		Sarvva Varma
600	Mahásena Gupta		Graha Varma
620	Mâdhava Gupta		Purna Varma
640	Aditya Sena D.		
660	Deva Gupta D.		
680	Vishnu Gupta D		
700	Jivita Gupta II.		

N.B.—Kumâra Gupta III. fought with Iṣâna Varma Maukhari. Mâdhava Gupta was contemporary with Harsha Vardhana.

N.B.—Avanti V. married Jaya Swâminî. Aditya V. married Harsha Guptâ. Iswara V. married Upa Guptâ (see Jaunpur inscript.).

COINS OF THE GUPTAS.

The coins of the Guptas form the most interesting series of all the Indian moneys. They are found in all three metals, gold, silver, and copper. The gold coins were the immediate successors of the Indo-Scythian Kushân dinârs in Northern India for several centuries, from A.D. 319, or perhaps even earlier, down to A.D. 600. The Guptas not only copied the types of the Kushân gold coins, but they adopted the same weight of about 123 grains, while they preserved the name of *Dinâr*, which had been introduced with the influx of Roman money. The coins of all the early kings give an average weight of 123 grains, of which 107 grains are pure; while 64 coins of the Kushân kings Wema Kadphises, Kanishka, Huvishka, and the earlier specimens of Vasu Deva give exactly the same average. The later coins of Vasu Deva show a falling off in the pure contents of nearly 10 grains.

But towards the end of Skanda Gupta's reign, the Gupta gold coins became much heavier, reaching an average of from 144 to 146 grains, while the pure contents were decreased to less than 70 grains. The coins of Nara Sinha Gupta of this standard are thus only one-half gold, and are, therefore, worth only two-thirds of the earlier Gupta dinars. A singular exception is the money of Prakâṣâditya, of a bright yellow colour, which contains 121·7 grains of pure metal out of 146. At present I cannot even guess the reason of this strange freak. The single coin of Jaya Gupta is still more debased, the pure contents being only one-fifth of its weight. I take it to belong to a much later date.

I add a table showing the weights and pure contents of the Gupta gold coins for comparison with those of their prototypes. The full weights were very steadily preserved, while the pure contents were slightly reduced from the 112·75 grains of the Indo-Scythians to 107 grains, or by 5·75 grains. But after Skanda Gupta's time the debasement of the coin became very great, although the actual weight of the pieces was increased. Apparently an attempt was made to revive the old Indian *suvarna* of 16 *mâshas* weight, or from 144 to 146 grains. But although the revival of the old Hindu name for the gold coin may have been a popular measure, the actual value of the coin was much less, being only two-thirds of those of the earlier Gupta kings of 123 grains, with 107 grains pure.

WEIGHTS OF GOLD COINS.

	Roman.	Weight.			
	Augustus—full wt., $\frac{1}{40}$ libra	126·25	pure		
	Do. Letronne . .	121·94	pure		
	Do. Brit. Mus. .	121·26	pure		
	Indo-Scythians.	means.	pure.	alloy.	
7	Wêma Kadphises . .	123·0	112·75	10·25	
11	Kanishka	123·0	112·75	10·25	
25	Huvishka	123·0	112·75	10·25	
21	Vasu Deva . . .	123·0	102·95	20·05	
64	**Later Indo-Scythians.**		pure.	alloy.	
	Kaneshki-*Viru* . . .	123·0	112·75	10·25	
	Shâka-*Mi*	123·0	107·62	15·38	
	Yellow *Kidar* . . .	120·0	105·00	15·00	
	Pale *Kidar* . . .	124·0	62·00	62·00	
	Late—pale Shâhi . .	120·0	75·00	45·00	
	Guptas.		pure.	alloy.	highest weights.
8	Kâcha	123	102·5	20·5	118·5
12	Chandra Gupta I. . .	123	107·6	15·4	123·8
50	Samudra Gupta . . .	123	107·6	15·4	126·0
40	Chandra Gupta II. . .	123	107·6	15·4	126·5
47	Kumâra Gupta I. . .	123	107·6	15·4	126·7
48	Skanda Gupta . . .	124·6	108·4	16·2	129·5
9	Do., pale heavy . . .	140	73·0	67·0	
4	Narasinha Gupta . .	146	73·0	73·0	147·0
2	Kumâra Gupta II. . .	148	66·5	81·5	150·0
2	Vishnu Gupta . . .	149	66·5	82·5	150·0
8	Saşângka	146	61·3	84·7	147·0
1	Jaya Gupta . . .	140	28·0	112·0	
	Prakâşaditya . . .	146	121·7		

The silver coins of the Guptas were copied from the silver money of the Western Satraps for their weight and fabric, and in the king's head on the obverse. On the reverse, however, a peacock was substituted for the Chaitya. The Gupta silver money begins with the coins of Chandra Gupta II. Vikramâditya. There are two different types of the peacock on the reverse. The Western coins of Mâlwa and Surâshtra show the bird standing to the front with outspread wings; while the northern coins of the Gangetic provinces show the peacock with extended wings and expanded tail. The northern coins also bear dates in the Gupta era, of which I believe the specimen of Chandra Gupta II., in Plate II. fig. 9, has the date of 80 odd. The weights of the coins vary from 29 to 36 grains, which shows that they, as well as their prototypes, the Satrap coins, were copied from the hemidrachms of the Greek kings of Kabul.

It is specially worthy of notice that on all the silver coins of the Guptas the head of the king invariably faces to the right, while on the silver coins of their foes, the White Hun Toramâna, and the Maukhari Iṣâna Varma, the head of the king faces to the left. This peculiarity was noted independently by Mr. Thomas and myself as probably indicating a different line of rulers. But Mr. Vincent Smith[5] "attaches no importance to the circumstance that the king's head is turned to the left, because," as he says, "the Gupta gold series prove that it was a matter of indifference which way the king's effigy was turned." But he has overlooked the fact that the gold coins of the king shooting a lion with the bow held in the

[5] *Journal Royal Asiatic Society*, 1889, p. 136.

right hand are probably only a blunder of the die-sinker. If not a blunder, then these Gupta kings must have been *ambidextrous* for several generations, as they are also represented shooting with the bow held in the *left* hand. But against this conclusion I may note the fact that, when the Gupta kings are shown with the end of the bow resting on the ground, they *invariably* hold it in the *left* hand.

As an illustration of an artist's blunder, I may cite a case which is within my own experience. An engraver with a photograph of Buddha before him actually copied it without reversing it, and consequently made Buddha appear with his *left* shoulder bare! If any copy of the first engraving should hereafter be found, it may perhaps be quoted as a proof that Buddha was sometimes represented with the *left* shoulder bare.

GUPTAS.

PLATE II. No.	Metal.	Grs.	
			NARA-SINHA GUPTA. A.D. 500—530.
1	AV	147	Author, rude execution, and pale metal. *King standing* to left, bow in left hand; right hand extended. Under left arm *Nara;* between feet *Gu.* *Lakshmi seated* on Lotus throne; legend to right, *Sri Balâditya.* N.B.—I give this coin because Mr. Vincent Smith thinks that there is "no authority" for reading Gu, which I take to stand for Gupta.
			KUMARA-GUPTA II.
2	AV	147	Author, rude execution and pale metal. *King standing* to left with bow; under left arm *Ku.* Lakshmi seated on Lotus throne; legend, *Sri Kramâditya.*

PLATE II.

GUPTAS AND NINE NAGAS.

PLATE II.

No.	Metal.	Grs.	
			JAYA-GUPTA.
3	AV	139	Author, rude execution ; pale gold. King standing to left, with bow in left hand ; sun standard to right. Under left arm *Jaya.* Lakshmi seated on throne ; legend, *Sri Prakâlâya* (?).
			VISHNU-GUPTA.
4	AV	149	Author. Pale metal, from Gaya ; duplicates in Brit. Mus. ; pale gold. King standing to left, under left arm *Vishnu.* Lakshmi seated on throne ; legend, *Sri Chandrâditya.*
			SASANGKA.
5	AV	145	Author. Gaya ; and duplicate from As. Soc., Bengal ; pale gold. Siva seated on Bull ; legend below, *Jaya.* Lakshmi seated on throne ; legend to right, *Ṣri Ṣaṣângka.*
6	Æ	41	Author, from *Ahichhatra.* *Buddha's Bowl,* surrounded by Buddhist railing. Indian legend [*Sri*] *Mahârâja* [*Ha*] *ri Guptasya.* The form of the letter *h* is peculiar to the Guptas.
7			Cornelian seal from Ariana Antiqua [Pl. I., fig. 4, page 51] ; legend wrongly read by Wilson ; rightly by Prinsep. *Female Bust,* with hand holding flower. Indian legend, *Keṣava-dâsasya*=" Slave of *Vishnu.*"
8	Æ	87	Author, 0·85 inch ; from Ahichhatra. The largest copper coin of the Guptas yet found. Female bust to left, with flower in right hand. *Garuda* symbol or standard of the Guptas ; legend lost.

PLATE II. No.	Metal.	Grs.	CHANDRA-GUPTA II.
9	Æ	29	Author, from Ajudhya, in Oudh. *Head of King* to right, numeral for 80 in front of face. *Peacock* standing to front with outstretched wings. Indian legend incomplete, *rájadhiraja Sri Chandra Gupta.*
10	Æ	36	Author. *Head of King* to right. Therefore a Gupta king. Peacock with expanded wings and tail. Legend in rather rude letters, *Vijit-âvanir-avanipati Sri* [*Skando*] *Gupto deva jayati.* Skando is Mr. Fleet's reading, which I think is very doubtful, as the coin must be of later date.
			TORAMÂṆA—WHITE HUN.
11	Æ	38	British Museum, with a duplicate. *Head of King* to left; date in front of face, 52. Rude peacock with expanded wings and tail. *Vijit-âvanir-avanipati Sri Toramâna deva-janita.*
			ISÂNA VARMA—MAUKHARI.
12	Æ	35	Author, two specimens from Ahichhatra. *Head of King*, facing to left; date in front of face, not read. Peacock with expanded wings and tail. Indian legend, *Vijit-âvanir-avanipati Sri Iṣána Varma.*

NARWAR.

The great fortress of Narwar was one of the State prisons of the Mogul Emperors. It is situated in a bend of the Sindh River, on an isolated hill upwards of four hundred feet in height. It is just fifty miles to the S.S.W. of Gwalior, and the same distance to the W.N.W. of Jhânsi. It derives its name from the famous Raja Nala, who is said to have been its builder. But as *nala*, "water-lily," is often used as a synonym for *Padma*, or "the lotus," I think that *Nalapura* is only another name for Padmâvati, which, as I shall presently show, was certainly an old name of the present city.

As I obtained all my principal coins of the Nâgas at Narwar, I have identified their capital of Padmâvati with that famous fortress. My account was published in 1865,[6] and as I have nothing to add to my description I will quote my original statements.

"In the *Vishnu Purâna* it is stated that 'the Nine Nâgas will reign in Padmâvati, Kantipuri, and Mathurâ, and the Guptas of Magadha along the Ganges to Prayâga.' This statement is corroborated by the *Vayu Purâna*, which, however, gives a second dynasty of Nâgas. 'The Nine Naka Kings will possess the city Champâvati, and the seven Nakas the pleasant city Mathurâ.' Princes of the Gupta race will possess all these countries, the banks of the Ganges to Prayâga, Saketa, and Magadha." [7]

Padmâvati was at first identified by H. H. Wilson with some unknown city in Berar, far to the south of the Narbadâ, and afterwards with Bhâgalpur on the Ganges; but the mention of Mathurâ utterly precludes the possibility of either of those places having belonged to the Nine Nâgas. Both cities should no doubt be looked for within some moderate distance of Mathurâ. The scene of Bhavabhuti's Mâlatî and Mâdhava is laid in the city of Padmâvati in the Vindhyan mountains. H. H. Wilson:—

"How wide the prospect spreads—mountain and rock,
Towns, villages, and woods, and glittering streams—
There where the *Pârâ* and the *Sindhu* wind,

---

[6] *Journal Bengal Asiatic Society.*

[7] H. H. Wilson's *Vishnu Purâna*, p. 479.

The towers and temples, pinnacles and gates,
And spires of *Padmávati*, like a city
Precipitated from the skies, appear
Inverted in the pure translucent wave."

Here the *Sindhu* River is clearly the *Sindh*, on which Narwar is situated, and the Pârâ River is the *Pârbati* or *Pârâ*, which flows only five miles to the north of the Sindh. The subsequent mention of the *Madhumati* and the *Luvana* as streams in the neighbourhood of the city, further confirms the identification, as the first must be the *Mohwar* or *Madhuwar* on the south, and the other the *Lûn* or *Nûn* to the north. Bhavabhuti further places the "holy shrine of *Swarna-Vindu*" near the frontier of the Madhumati and Sindhu, which may be identified with *Suhenda*, or *Sonabindu*=*Sonenda*, which is close by.

The identification of Narwar with Padmâvati is supported by the mention on the Allahabad Pillar of *Ganapati-Nâga* among the Rajas tributary to Samudra Gupta. We know from extracts already given from the *Purânas* that the Nagas were contemporary with the Guptas, which is further proved by the similarity of their copper coins, which are mostly small pieces of 36, 18, and 9 grains. As contemporaries of the Guptas the Nine Nâgas must have reigned during the fourth and fifth centuries A.D.

As Kântipura and Mathurâ are included within their rule, their dominions probably extended over Bharatpur, Dholpur, Gwalior, and part of Bundelkhand. This was the country of Raja Nala. I feel inclined, therefore, to identify the Nâgas with some of the early Kachwâha Rajas of Gwalior and Narwar, amongst whom I find the names of *Bhîma*, *Vyâghra*, *Vasumitra*, and *Ganapati*. The later Kachwâhas, who claimed descent from Raja Nala, were certainly in possession of both places, as the name of the last of them, Dulha Deva, who founded the Kachwâha dynasty of Amber (Jaypur) is still attached to one part of the Fort of Narwar. He is recorded in the Jaypur chronicles to have been expelled from Gwalior and Narwar, and at Narwar itself he is said to have escaped from that part of the fort which still bears his name. (See James Prinsep's *Useful Tables*, quoting Tod's *Rajasthan*.)

THE NINE NAGAS OF NARWAR.

PLATE II. No.	Metal	Grs.	
			KHA ++.
13	Æ	50	Author, from Narwar; unique. Peacock standing to right. Two upright strokes; one with side piece; Indian legend incomplete, *Kha*.
			VA ++.
14	Æ	36	Author, from Narwar; unique. Peacock standing to right. Two upright strokes, as on No. 13. Indian legend incomplete, *Va*.
			BHIMA-NÂGA.
15	Æ	34·1	Author, from Narwar; 5 specimens. Peacock standing to left. Horizontal line like a spear-head. Indian legend in two horizontal lines: *Mahârâja Bhîma Nâga*.
			SKANDA-NÂGA.
16	Æ	34	Author, from Narwar; 12 specimens. Peacock standing to right. Two daggers, or short spears. Indian legend, *Mahârâja Skanda Nâgasya*.
17	Æ	50·1	Author, from Narwar. Recumbent humped Bull, in a circle of pellets. Two daggers. Indian legend, *Mahârâja Skanda Naga*.

PLATE II.

No.	Metal.	Grs.	
			BRIHASPATI NÂGA.
18	Æ	18·3	Author, from Narwar; 31 specimens. Recumbent humped Bull. Indian legend, *Mahârâja Brihaspati Nâga.*
			GANAPATI NAGA.
19	Æ	36	Author, from Narwar, Gohad, Doab. Very common; of 3 sizes, representing Kâkinis, 36 grains; half Kâkinis, 18 grains; quarter Kâkinis, 9 grains and 7 grains. Humped Bull walking to left. Indian legend, *Mahârâja Sri Ganapatya.* N.B.—The name on different coins varies both in form and spelling. On some it is written both *Ganendra* and *Ganendra.* The coins are extremely common, as I have seen several thousands of them.
20	Æ	17	Author. Humped Bull, and legend *Mahârâja Sri Ganendra.*
21	Æ	8	Author, same type and same legend.
			VYÂGHRA [NÂGA.]
22	Æ	18	Author. Half Kâkinis; very rare; square. Wheel surrounded by circle of pellets. *Rev.—Vyâghra* . .
			DEVA-NÂGA.
23	Æ	36	Author. *Kâkini.* Humped Bull walking to right; circle of pellets. *Trisul of Siva.* Indian legend, *Mahârâja Sri Deva Nâgasya.*
24	Æ	26	Author. *Kâkini;* 18 Kakinis and 2 half Kakinis. Wheel, in circle of pellets. *Rev.*—Indian legend, *Mahârâja Sri Deva Nâgasya.*
25	Æ	17	Author. *Half Kâkini;* unique. Trisul of Siva in circle of pellets. *Rev.*—Indian legend as on last.

III.—Hindu Coinage of Kashmir.

The Hindu Kingdom of Kashmir, even in its most palmy days, never extended beyond the limits of the Alpine Panjab. In the seventh century, when the Chinese pilgrim Hwen Thsang visited the valley, all the hilly country between the Indus and the Jhelam Rivers belonged to Kashmir, and this extension of the kingdom is well marked by the still existing temples at Amb, Mallot, Ketâs, and Bâghanwâla in the Salt Range, which are all in the Kashmirian style of architecture. The influence of Kashmir was of course felt more or less by all the smaller hill states. The submission of the two southern states Punach (or Purnotsa) and Rajaori (or Râjapuri) was the most permanent, but that of the more distant states of Champa (or Champapuri) and Trigartta (or Kangra) was little more than nominal at any time. I have, indeed, a very strong suspicion that the extension of the kingdom in the seventh century was due rather to the conquest of the valley of Kashmir itself, by the rulers of the ancient province of Taxila, than to the annexation of Taxila by Kashmir. The native chronicles speak of successful expeditions to Nepâl, Mâlwa, and Southern India, and even to Ceylon. But the last was probably only the quibbling result of some vain boast that kept the word of promise to the ear by referring to a small island in the lake of Kashmir, which still bears the name of Lanka (or Ceylon). Like Bengal, Kashmir was never a conquering power. As Maharaja Gulâb Singh replied to me when I asked him whether he had any Kashmiris in his army, "*Kuchh kâm-kâ nahîn,*" "They are useless."

Of the early history of Kashmir little is known beyond the bare facts that the valley in the third century B.C.

formed part of the great empire of Asoka, and that in the early centuries A.D., it belonged to the wide dominions of the Kushân Indo-Scythians, Kanishka, Huvishka, and Vâsu Deva. Intermediately it must certainly have been tributary to the Indo-Greek Princes Menander and his successors, although there is no allusion to them in the native chronicles. In the beginning of the sixth century, when the power of the Little Kushâns was overthrown by the White Huns, the valley was seized by the powerful Ephthalite Prince Mihirkul, and his coins are amongst the earliest specimens of Kashmir money. I possess also one coin of *Khingila*, or Narendrâditya, one of the recorded successors of Mihirkul. The type of his coin is the same as that of Mihirkul, while his name of *Khingila* betrays his foreign origin, his other name of *Narendrâditya* being only his Indian title, or perhaps a translation of his Scythian name. All these coins are described in my account of the White Huns, which will be published in the *Numismatic Chronicle*.

In the beginning of the seventh century the throne of Kashmir fell to Durlabha, whose reputed father was a *Nâga* or serpent. He founded the dynasty which was called the *Karkotaka*, or *Nâga-vamsi*, and with him begins the first regular series of Kashmirian coins. In A.D. 713 his grandson, *Chandra-pira* (*Chin-to-lo-pi-li*), applied to the Emperor of China for aid against the Arabs,[8] whose army in that very year, under Muhammad Kâsim, after the conquest of Sindh, had advanced to the foot of the Kashmir hills. Durlabha himself is, I believe, also mentioned by the Chinese[9] under the name of *Chu-lo-pa*, as an Indian

---

[8] Remusat, *Nouveaux Mélanges Asiatiques*, i., 197.
[9] *Ibid.*, i., 212.

king who, between A.D. 627 and 645, was required to aid the envoys from *Kipin*, or Arakhosia, on their way back from China. This statement shows that Kashmir was then one of the acknowledged routes between India and China.

The earliest coins that can be assigned with certainty to a Kasmirian king are of several different types, all of which bear the well-known name of Mihirkul, the great Ephthalite conqueror. His silver pieces are copied from the thin Sassanian coinage of middle age. On the obverse is the king's head with the *trisul* of Siva behind the royal standard, surmounted by Siva's Bull in front of the face. The legend in Indian letters is *Jayatu-Mihira-kula*. A second silver coin of similar type has the legend, *Jayatu Vrisha-dhwaja*, "May the Bull-standard be victorious." These silver coins are extremely rare. The small copper coins are of a similar kind. On the obverse is the king's head with the Indian legend, *Sri Mihira-kula;* and on the reverse a humped bull, with the Indian legend, *Jayatu Vrisha*, "May the Bull be victorious." The larger copper coins are of the Kushân type, with the standing king and the seated goddess. On these coins there are two different legends, both being in Indian characters. The one is *Jayatu Mihira-kula*, and the other is *Shâhi Mihira-gula*. The former, I conclude, was struck in Kashmir, the latter either in *Gandhâra* or in Taxila. A third class of copper coins is of still larger size, with a horseman on the obverse, and the Indian legend *Mihira-kula*, sometimes written in the wrong direction from right to left.

The next class of coins includes the names of *Toramâna* and his son *Pravarasena*, both of whom belonged to the recorded members of the royal family of Kashmir. On all these coins there is the additional name of *Kidâra*, written perpendicularly, from which I infer that they were of the tribe of Little Kushâns, the descendants of *Kidâra*. This inference is strengthened by the fact that I possess three silver coins of a king with the legend *Kidâra Kushâna Shâhi*, "Kidâra, King of the Kushâns." These are described in my account of the "Coins of the Little Kushâns," recently published in the *Numismatic Chronicle*.

The kingdom of the *Little Yueti*, or *Little Kushâns*, was established at *Fu-leu-sha* (*Purusha*, or Peshâwur) by *Ki-to-lo*, or *Kidâra*, King of the Kushâns or *Great Yue-ti*. Being recalled to protect his own dominions against the White Huns, he left his son behind in Gandhâra, who thus became the King of the Little Kushâns. Five districts to the north of Gandhâra belonged to him.[10] These would have included *Udyâna* and *Bajâwar* to the west of the Indus, and Darvâbhisâra to the east of the river. This settlement must have taken place shortly after the permanent occupation of the valley of the Oxus by the White Huns, about the middle of the fifth century A.D. In 520 A.D., the Chinese pilgrim Sung Yun found the Ephthalite King of Gandhâra at war with Kipin (Arakhosia), and discontented with the small extent of his territory. To the descendants of Kidâra, therefore, I would ascribe the conquest of Kashmir, which the Gakkars now claim for their King *Kid*, or *Kaid*. This would account satisfactorily for the occurrence of the name of *Kidâra* on so many of the coins of Kashmir and the North-Western Panjâb before the accession of the Karkotaka or Nâga dynasty under Durlabha in A.D. 625.

The name of *Kitolo* is still preserved in these western

---

[10] Remusat, *Nouvelles Mélanges Asiatiques*, i., 224. See also *Les Huns Blancs*, par Viv. de St. Martin, p. 44.

countries by the rulers of Chitrâl and Gilgit, who proudly style themselves *Shah-Kitor*.

The coins of the Kârkotaka or Nâga dynasty are of very bold but rude workmanship. They are apparently intended for gold *dinârs*, but the gold is always more or less alloyed with silver. The alloy is sometimes so much as to make it difficult to say whether the pieces contain any gold at all. There are also specimens in copper of the same types; but most of these appear to me to be simple forgeries that have been originally gilt. There were, however, *copper dinârs*, as it is recorded that the Raja *Jayapiṛa* (A.D. 760—780) having found a copper mine, struck one hundred *kotis*, less one, of dinârs in his own name. It is also said that he gave to an eminent Pandit named Bhaṭṭa, an allowance of one *lakh* (100,000) dinârs daily.[11] As these coins weigh 120 and 121 grains, they are the direct descendants of the gold dinârs of the Kushân Princes Kanishka and Huvishka in weight as well as in type, although the type is miserably degraded.

The next dynasty of Kashmir princes was founded by *Avanti-Varma* in A.D. 855. From this time the dates have been carefully registered in the Raja Tarangini, or Sanskrit Chronicles of Kashmir; and the succession of princes is very completely illustrated by their coins. The same types, also, which had been originally adopted from the Indo-Scythian money, were continued down to the end. The only difference, in fact, is the more complete

[11] *Raja Tarangini*, iv., *sl.* 616. He struck one thousand millions, less one, of inârs of copper. The daily allowance of one *lakh* (100,000) of dinars to the "excellent Bhaṭṭa" must certainly have been in this copper currency.—*Raja Tarangini*, iv., *sl.* 495.

degradation of the figures of both the Raja and the Goddess, which are only recognisable by tracing them back to their originals. Thus the same types had actually remained in use for upwards of one thousand years.

Gopâla Varma, the second king of the Varma dynasty, was a conqueror, and he added the district of Gujarât to the Kashmir dominions. Both his father *Avanti-Varma* and himself were builders of temples. His father built the grand temples at Avantipura, which still exist in ruins; and in his own reign the massive temples at Pathan were erected by his queen, Sugandha Ranî.[12] All these temples have been described in my account of the Temples of Kashmir published in the *Journal of the Bengal Asiatic Society* for 1848.

Monetary System of Kashmir.

Upwards of fifty years ago I wrote an account of the Coinage of Kashmir, published in the *Numismatic Chronicle* for 1843. I then made known the coins of seventeen different Hindu princes which I had obtained in the valley in 1839. But the lapse of time has gradually increased my collection, and I am now able to bring forward the coins of no less than thirty-eight different Hindu kings of Kashmir, who reigned from the sixth to the thirteenth century, A.D. Some of these coins are now exceedingly common, but others are very rare, and a few are still unique. Most of the known coins are of copper; but the existence of a few specimens, both of gold and of silver, proves that there must have been a coinage of both of these metals, and gives a hope that more specimens may

[12] *Raja Tarangini*, v., 157.

yet be found. Gold coins named *Rupaka*[13] are mentioned in the reign of Yaṣaskara, A.D. 940, but their value is not known. The dictionaries say that the Rupaka was one-seventieth of a Suvarṇa, which seems an almost impossible subdivision. As the Suvarṇa was a coin of about 144 grains, the Rupaka would have been a small piece of only 2·057 grains, which seems too small for any real coin. Both gold and silver coins are spoken of in the reign of Harsha Deva, A.D. 1090, as the chief money of commerce, while the copper coin was but little used. I have specimens of the gold coins of different types, weighing 73 and 72 grains, and one of silver weighing 23·5 grains.

The only account of the monetary system of Kashmir that I have met with is a short notice by Abul Fazl in the *Ain-Akbari*. The following is his description of the coins in use in the time of Akbar :—

2	Bârahkânis, or "Twelvers"	= 1	Panchi, or "Twenty-fiver," or Kasirah.
4	Panchis,[14] or "Twenty-fivers"	= 1	Hăt, or "Hundreder," or Râhat.
10	Hăts, or "Hundreders"	= 1	Sâsnu, or "Thousander."
1¼	Sâsnu	= 1	Rab-sâsnu or Rop-sâsnu, or Sikkah.

The *Panchi* was also known by the name of *Kasira*, that is, the "brass or copper coin."
The *Hăt* was equal to 1 *Dâm* of Akbar, or $\frac{1}{40}$th of a rupee.
The *Sâsnu* was equal to 10 Dâms, or ¼ rupee.

The values and weights of the different coins are easily deducible from Abul Fazl's account; thus :—

The *Panchi* or *Kasira*, which was equal to ¼ *dâm*,

---

[13] In the *Ain Akbari*, Jarrett, ii., 354, the rop-sâsnu is said to be a silver coin.

[14] *Panchhu.*

according to this account, must have weighed about 80 grains, or ¼ of 320 grains. But the greater number of my copper coins range from 85 to 95 grains each, the average of 30 good specimens of 30 different kings being 91 grains, while two half coins, or *Bârakânis* of Kshema Gupta, weigh 45 grains each. The copper coins of the Muhammadan kings are somewhat lighter, the average being only 83 grains.

Of the Hindu silver coins very few specimens have come down to us. I possess only one specimen of Raja Harsha Deva, which weighs 23·5 grains. As this would be equal to only one-eighth of a rupee, or 5 dâms, its value must have been 5 *hăts* of Kashmir, or one half *sâsnu*. But my Muhammadan silver coins, of which I have weighed 28 specimens, give an average of 94 grains, which I take to represent a double *sâsnu*, or 4 half *sâsnus*. The SILVER coinage must therefore have been as follows :—

½ Sâsnu	= 5 Hăts	= 22·4 grs.	=1 Kona, or ½ Kârsha	
1 Sâsnu	=10 Hăts	= 44·8 grs.	=1 Kârsha	[punch marked]
1 Rab-Sâsnu	=15 Hăts	= 67·2 grs.	=1 Drachma	[Greek]
2 Sâsnus	=20 Hăts	= 89·6 grs.	=2 Kârshas.	

For *Rab-sâsnu* the Kasmirian Pandits now read *Rop-sâsnu*, or the "silver *sâsnu*," as Abul Fazl, in the *Ain-Akbari*, says it was a silver coin of 9 *mâshas*. As the *mâsha* of silver was only 2 *ratis* (or *surkhs*) in weight; the *Rop-sâsnu* of 9 *mâshas* would have been 1·82 × 2 × 9 = 32·76 grains in weight. But I presume that the *mâsha* of 5 or 6 *ratis* (or *surkhs*) is intended, and if so, the weight would be 1·82 × 6 = 10·92 grains for the *mâsha*, or 1·82 × 5 = 9·10 grains. In this case, the weight of the *Rop-sâsnu* would be either 98·28 grains or 81·9 grains. But the true weight of the coin can readily be calculated from its value of 15 *hăts*, or 15 *dâms*, that is $\frac{15}{40}$ of a rupee. Taking the rupee at $179\frac{1}{3}$ grains of pure silver, the *Rop-sâsnu* would be $\frac{179\frac{1}{3}}{40} \times 15 = 67.25$ grains, or exactly equal to the Greek drachma. My silver coin of Harsha Deva (Pl. V. fig. 23), of 23·5 grains, is therefore one-third of a *Rop-sâsnu*, or 22·4 grains. It was therefore a half *sâsnu*. And these three—the half *sâsnu*, the *sâsnu*, and the *Rop-sâsnu*—must have formed the silver coinage of Kashmir.

The large silver coin of Pravarasena (Pl. III. fig. 4), which weighs 120 grains, would therefore have been a piece of $2\frac{1}{2}$ *sâsnus*, or 25 *hăts*.

In connection with these coins I should expect to find a gold piece of 25 *sâsnus*. This should be 44·8 grains × 25 = 1120, which, as 8 *ratis* of silver = 1 of gold, gives a gold piece of 140 grains, that is, the Indian *suvarna*. No piece of this size has yet been found, but my two gold coins of Harsha Deva, which weigh 73 and 72 grains, must be *half-suvarnas*.

The money of Kashmir, as described in the following pages, consisted of the following denominations, the names of the existing coins being distinguished by capital letters.

GOLD.—*Suvarnas*, and HALF-SUVARNAS.
SILVER.—*Rop-Sâsnus*, *Sâsnus*, and HALF-SÂSNUS.
COPPER.—PANCHIS, or KASIRAS, and HALF-PANCHIS.

I have found nothing to indicate the value of the *white metal* coins that were issued by Didda Râni, Sangrâma, Ananta, and Kalasa, from A.D. 980 to 1080. (Pl. V. fig. 20.) They are clearly a distinct coinage, better than copper, and less valuable than silver. I conjecture that they may have been intended for *hăts*, each equal to 5 *panchis* or copper coins. They would thus have taken the place of silver, and would account for the scarcity of silver coins in the Kashmir series.

Several kinds of coins are mentioned in the Kashmir history. The earliest are the copper *dinârs* of Toramâṇa. As the younger brother of the reigning king Hiranya, he presumed to call in all the former money called *Bâlâ-hat*, and to strike *dinârs* in his own name.[15] *Hăt* means "struck," and is therefore used for coin in general, but as *hat* was the special name of a particular coin or "the hundreder" in Kashmir, I believe that the old coins here referred to were the Indo-Scythian copper money which had continued in use down to that time. Their weight is the same as that of the common Indo-Scythian coins, such as those of Hiranyakula, Mihirakula, Gokarna, and others.

In the reign of Raja Ananta mention is made of a jewelled "lingam" which his queen sold for 70 *lakhs* of *takkas*. As *tangha*, or *takka*, was the common name for a copper coin, I have little doubt that the pieces here referred to are the well-known copper *panchis*, or $\frac{1}{4}$ *hats*, of Ananta Raja, each equal to $\frac{1}{160}$ of a rupee. The whole amount would therefore be not much over £40,000. It is *possible*, however, that the *white metal* pieces of Ananta may have been called *tankas*.

In the reign of Harsha Deva his gold coins were copied from those of Karnâta in South India. They were called *Utkosha*, which means simply "fine gold."[16]

---

[15] *Raja Tarangini*, iii., 103.

[16] *Ibid.*, v. [The reference is incomplete in the manuscript, and I have been unable to supply it. There is probably some mistake here. I have been unable to find the word *Utkosha* either in the Rājataranginī or in any of the dictionaries.—E. J. R.]

But the fact of the coins being made in imitation of those of Karnâta is fully corroborated by the coins of that country. Sir Walter Elliot has referred these coins to Konga-desa, or Coimbatore, but the curious fact just quoted proves that they must belong to *Karnâta*, or the Carnatic.

The unit of the Kashmir money account was the KÂNI of 2 *surkhs* or *ratis*, 1·82 grains × 2 = 3·64 grains. Twelve and a half *kânis* made one Bârah-kâni, or "twelver"; twenty-five *kânis* made a *panchi*, or "twenty-fiver"; and one hundred *kânis* made a *hăt*, or "hundreder." In Kashmir and the Punjâb the Sanskrit *ṣat* = 100 is pronounced *hat*. Hence the name of the coin. The *panchi* was a copper coin, equal in value to one quarter of a *dâm* of Akbar's money. It was also called *kasira*, or "the copper." The *hat* was equal to 1 *dâm*. The *sâsnu* was equal to 10 *hats*, from *sahasra*, or "one thousand" contracted to *sâs*.

	Surkh or Rati.	KANI.	Shakri.	BÂRAHKANI.	PANCHI.	HAT.	½ Sâsnu.	SÂSNU.	ROP-SÂSNU.	DOUBLE SÂSNU.	Grains.
COPPER.	1										1·82
	2	1									3·64
		3⅛	1								11·20
		12½	4	1							45·50
		25	8	2	1						91·00
		100	32	8	4	1					364
SILVER.					20	5	1				22·4
					40	10	2	1			44·8
					60	15	3	1½	1		67·2
					80	20	4	2	1⅓	1	89·6

Coin Types.

The constant type of the Kashmir coinage, the standing Raja and the sitting Goddess, was adopted from the money of the Indo-Scythian Kushân kings, Kanishka, Huvishka, and Vasu Deva. It was the common type also of the great Gupta dynasty of India from its adoption by Samudra Gupta in the middle of the fourth century A.D. On the earliest certain specimens of the Kashmir kings—the coins of Mihirkul, Hiranyakul, Gokarna, and others,—the king is represented as standing to the front with his face turned towards the left. His left hand holds a spear upright, and his right hand is stretched out over a small object which is supposed to be an altar. On the reverse there is a seated goddess, named *Ardoksho* on the Indo-Scythian coins, who holds a cornucopiæ in her left hand, and a royal fillet or diadem in her right hand. On these coins *Ardoksho* represents the "earth goddess." On the Hindu coins of the Guptas she becomes gradually identified with the goddess *Lakshmi*, holding a lotus in her left hand instead of a cornucopiæ. On the coins of Toramâṇa and his son Pravarasena the cornucopiæ is replaced by the lotus; but on the later coins the arms of the goddess are gradually displaced by the letters of the inscription. At first the left arm is omitted, as on the coins of Sankara Varma and Gopâla Varma; but on the later coins the right arm gives place to the title of *Sri*, which precedes most of the names. But the types rapidly become more and more degraded until it is difficult to trace them back to their originals.

The only new types in the Kashmir series were those introduced by Harsha Deva for his gold and silver coins. The "elephant" type, which he used for both metals [Pl. V., figs. 22, 23], was copied from the coins of Karnâta, and the "Horseman" type [Pl. V., fig. 21] was imitated from the money of the Brâhmani kings of Kabul [see Pl. VII.—Gandâra].

The standard coin type of Kashmir thus remained unchanged from the type of Kanishka in A.D. 78, down to the Muhammadan conquest in A.D. 1339, or for 1261 years. Of course the types became so very much degraded that it is difficult to say which figure is intended for the standing king and which for the sitting goddess on the coins of Jaga Deva and Raja Deva of the thirteenth century. The Kashmir coinage therefore offers an almost unique example of a coin type remaining unchanged for upwards of twelve centuries.

CHRONOLOGY.

The following lists of the kings of Kashmir are taken from the *Raja Tarangini*, a Sanskrit history begun by Kalhana Pandita, and continued by other writers down to the Muhammadan conquest. All the early part is little better than a mere list of names, amongst which we find *Asoka*, and the Indo-Scythian princes *Hushka*, *Jushka*, and *Kanishka*. Still later there is mention of *Mihirakul*, who conquered the country. But he was certainly the great king of the White Huns who overran the whole of Northern India in the beginning of the sixth century A.D. He was therefore the paramount sovereign under whom the Raja of Kashmir was only a tributary prince.

The real history of the Kashmir kings begins with the Yuva Raja *Toramâna* and his son *Pravarasena*, of both of whom we have coins. Shortly after them comes *Durlabha*, the founder of the *Nâga* dynasty, of whom also we have coins, as well as of many of his successors. The actual dates begin with the death of Vrihaspati of the Nâga dynasty in the year 89 of the *Lok-kâl*, or A.D. 813. The lengths of reigns only are given of the earlier dynasties, and all the previous chronology is simply absurd. For instance, the names of paramount sovereigns of the Kushâns and White Huns are mixed up with those of the tributary rulers of Kashmir. Thus, Meghavâhan, the grandson of Yudhishthira, is said to have been protected by Gopâditya, King of Gandhâra ; but the interval between Gopâditya and Meghavâhan consists of three reigns covering 130 years, besides a whole separate dynasty of 192 years, making altogether 222 years! Then again Gopâditya is placed 300 years after Mihirkul, making the period between Mihirkul and Meghavâhan upwards of 500 years ; whereas we know that Mihirkul reigned about 515 to 540 A.D., while Pravarasena, the grandson of Meghavâhan, could not have been later than fifty years after him.

The chronology of the Nâga dynasty in the early reigns, as given in the *Raja Tarangini*, is certainly wrong by about thirty years, as shown by some dates recorded in the Chinese annals, of which the three following dates are examples.

I. *Chandrapiṛa*, the grandson of the founder, is placed in A.D. 696—699. According to the Chinese, the Raja of Kashmir, named *Chin-to-lo-pi-li*, applied to the Emperor of China in A.D. 713 for aid against the Arabs—and, II. his successor, his younger brother *Mu-to-pi-li* [or *Mukta-piṛa*] was on the throne in A.D. 720.[17]

III. Another notice by the Chinese seems to refer to *Durlabha* himself. Between the years A.D. 627—649, the King of India, named *Tu-lo-pa*, was charged to have the envoys from Kipin safely conducted to their own country.[18]

---

[17] Remusat, *Nouvelles Mélanges Asiatiques*, i., 197.
[18] *Ibid.*, i., 212.

As Kashmir lay in the route to Kipin I conclude that *Tu-lo-pa* must be Durlabha.

Guided by these three dates I propose to correct Durlabha's accession by thirty-one years, or from A.D. 594, to A.D. 625. I select this date as it is the first year of the centenary cycle of the Lok-kâl, which came into use in Kashmir during the reign of the Nâga dynasty. I place the accession of Chandrapiṛa in A.D. 711, and his application to China for aid in 713, when Muhammad Kâsim was in the Northern Panjab.

The following lists of Rajás are taken from the *Raja Tarangini*, beginning with Meghavâhan, the grandfather of Toramâna and Pravarasena—whose dates are only approximate, although they cannot be far from the truth. This family must have belonged to the Little Kushâns, as their coins bear the name of *Kidâra, i.e. Ki-tol*, the founder of the Little Yue-ti. There are ten names in the list, to which I have added the years of each king as recorded in the *Raja Tarangini*, together with the probable dates of some of them according to my judgment.

Probable date. A.D.		Reign. Years.	
480	Meghavâhan	34	
500	Sreshtasena	30	
520	Hiranya	30	brothers.
	Toramâna . .		
	Matrigupta, a Brahman .	4	
540	Pravarasena . . .	60	
560	Yudhishthira . . .	21	
580	Narendrâditya . .	13	brothers.
	Ranâditya . . .	300 (*sic*)	
600	Vikramâditya . . .	42	brothers.
	Bâlâditya . . .	37	

NÂGA DYNASTY.

Reigns.	Probable Accession.	NAMES.	Generations.	TITLES.	Years' reign.	A.D.
	A.D.					
1	625	Durlabha .	I.		36	605
2	681	Pratâpaditya I.	II.		50	641
3	711	Chandrapiṛa	III.		8	691
4	—	Târapiṛa . .			4	699
5	719	Muktapiṛa .		Lalitâditya . . / Pratâpâditya II.	36[19]	703
6	745	Kuvalayapiṛa	IV.		1	739
7	746	Vajrâditya .		Vappiyaka . .	7	740
8	753	Prithivyapiṛa	V.		4	747
9	—	Sangrâmapiṛa		[only seven days.]	—	—
10	757	Jayapiṛa . . [Jajja]		Vinayâditya .	31	751
					—	—
11	782	Lalitapiṛa .	VI.		12	782
12	794	Sangrâmapiṛa		Prithivyapiṛa .	7	794
13	801	Vrihaspati .	VII.	Jayapiṛa . . .	12	801
14	813	Ajitapiṛa . .		Lok-kâl	89 =	813
15	849	Anangapiṛa .				849
16	852	Utpâlapiṛa .	VIII.			852
	855				31	855

[19] The Calcutta edition has 26 years. The *Raja Tarangini*, iv. 134, says that Lalitâditya obtained the name of Pratâpaditya.

The probable dates in this list have been derived from the corrections rendered necessary by the statements of the Chinese annals regarding *Chandrapiṛa* and *Muktapiṛa*, which place these kings in A.D. 713 and 720.

The period between Muktapiṛa's death in 745 and Vrihaspati's death in A.D. 813 is only 68, whereas by the lengths of the intervening reigns it is made 74 years. I have accordingly reduced Jayapiṛa's reign to 25 years tentatively to make the chronology agree with the dates.

The 16 names cover 230 years [from A.D. 625 to 855] or 8 generations, giving 14 years to a reign and 28 years to a generation.

Varma Dynasty.

	Accession. Lok-kal.	A.D.	NAMES.	
1	31	855	Avanti Varma	Aditya Varma
2	59	883	Sankara Varma	
3	77	901	Gopâla Varma	
4	79	903	Sankata V.	
5	79	903	Sugandhâ Râni	
6	89	905	Pârtha Varma	
7	97	921	Nirjita Varma	
8	98	922	Chakra Varma	
9	9	933	Sura Varma I.	
		934	Pârtha Varma	
	11	934	Chakra Varma	
10	11	935	Sankara Vardhana	
		936	Chakra V.	
11	13	937	Unmattâvanti	
12	15	939	Sura Varma II.	

Mixed Dynasties.

	Lok-kal.	A.D.	NAMES.	
1	15	939	Yaṣaskara	Yâskara
2	24	948	Sangrâma Deva	
3	24	949	Parva Gupta	
4	24	950	Kshema Gupta	
5	34	958	Abhimanyu Gupta	
6	48	972	Nandi Gupta	
7	49	973	Tribhuvana Gupta	
8	51	974	Bhîma Gupta	
9	56	979	Diddâ Rânî	
10	81	1005	Sangrâma Deva	
11	4	1028	Hari Raja	
12	4	1028	Ananta Deva	
13	57	1081	Kalasa	
14	65	1089	Harsha	
15	77	1101	Uchchala	
16	87	1111	Salhana	
17	88	1112	Sussala	
18	95	1120	Bhikshâcharya	

Mixed Dynasties—*continued.*

	Accession.		NAMES.	
	Lok-kal.	A.D.		
19	3	1127	Jaya Sinha Deva I.	
20	6	1130	Mallârjuna	
21	8	1132	Jaya Sinha Deva II.	
22		1155	Paramânak	
23		1164	Avanti Deva	
24		1171	Bhopya Deva	
25		1180	Jassa Deva	
26		1198	Jaga Deva	
27		1214	Raja Deva I.	
28		1236	Sangrâma Deva	
29		1254	Raja Deva II.	
30		1256	Lakshmana Deva	
31		1269	Kajjala	
32		1287	Sinha Deva	
33		1301	Rinchana	
34		1320	Udyâna Deva	
35	99	1323	Kota Rânî	
		1339	Muhammadan Conque	st

COINS OF KASHMIR.

PLATE III. No.	Metal.	Grs.	Toramâna.
1	Æ	101	Author, Duplicate Brit. Mus. ; very rare. *King standing* to left as on Indo-Scythian coins ; *Sri Turyamâna.* *Lakshmi* seated, with lotus in left hand. [*Ki*] *dâra* written perpendicularly to left.
2	Æ	113	*King standing* as on No. 1. Nimbus round head ; *Sri Toramâṇa* ; common. *Lakshmi seated* holding lotus in left hand, and right-hand raised ; *Kidara* written upright to left ; on some coins a lion's head below.

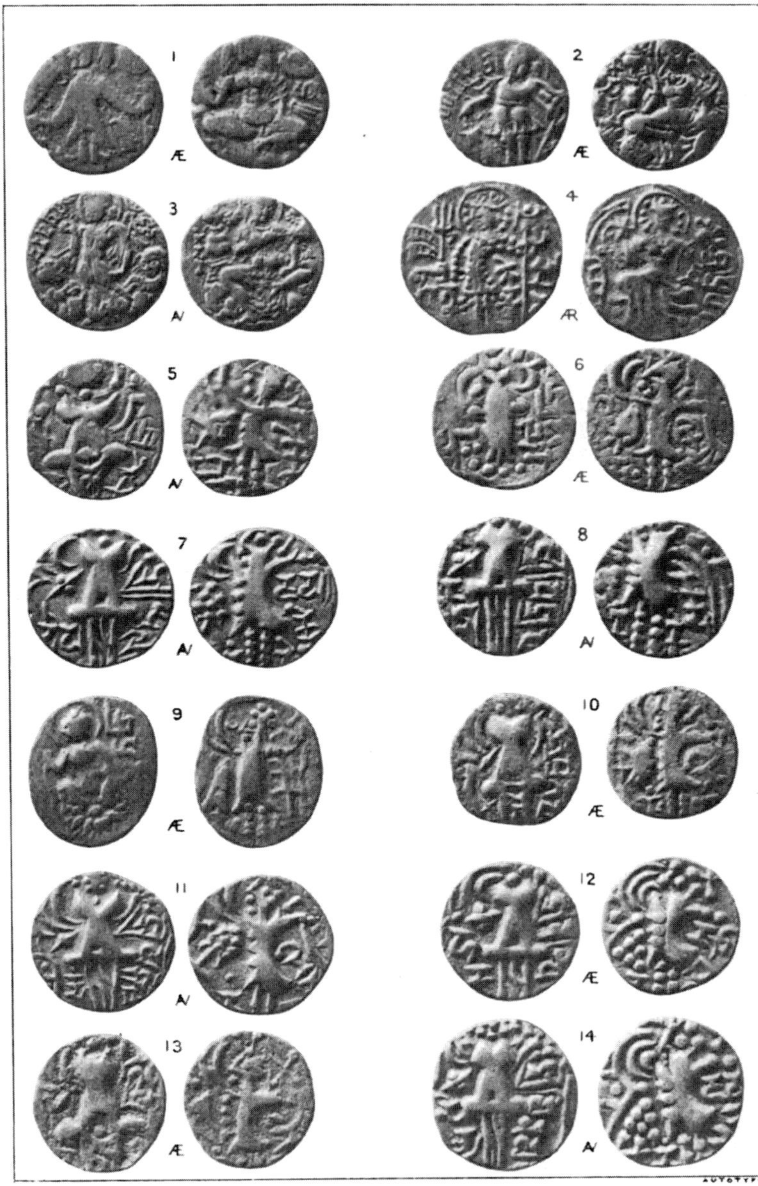

KASHMIR.

PLATE III.

No.	Metal.	Grs.	
			PRAVARASENA.
3	AV		Lady Clive Bayley, a well-preserved coin. *Raja standing* to front; left hand on hip; right hand raised; two figures seated below, on right and left; *Sri Pravara-sena.* *Lakshmi seated* on Lion; lotus in left hand; vase of flowers to left. Legend written perpendicularly on left, *Kidâra.*
4	AR	120	British Museum, 0·95 inch. *Lakshmi seated,* lotus in left hand; to right, *Sri Pravara.* *King standing* to left holding sceptre with crescent head in left hand; right hand extended; trisul above hand; to right, *Sena;* under left arm, *Kidâra;* to left below, *ratna* (?)
			NARENDRADITYA.
5	AV	115	Author, from Kuram valley; 2 specimens; very rude. *Rude figure of female* seated; to right, *Sri Narendra.* *Rude figure of Raja* standing; under arm, *Kidâ*[*ra*].
			GOKARNA.
6	Æ	107	Author, unique. Very rude figure of female seated; to right, *Sri Gokarṇa.* Very rude figure of Raja standing; under arm, *Kida*[*ra*].

NAGA DYNASTY.

			DURLABHA, A.D. 625.
7	AV	122	*Author.* Rude coin; apparently all the specimens are cast. Rude figure of Lakshmi seated; *Sri Durlabha:* and to left, *Deva.* Rude figure of Raja standing; *Jaya*[*ti*], and *Kidâra.*

PLATE III. No.	Metal.	Grs.	
			VIGRAHA [? VAJRA] A.D. 650.
8	AV	113	*Author*, very common. Types same as No 7. *Obv.*—*Sri Vigraha*; two letters to left not read. *Rev.*—*Kida*[*ra*]; double struck.
			PRATÂPÂDITYA I., A.D. 661.
9	Æ	101	Author, early type; unique. *Obv.*—Goddess seated; *Sri Pratâpa.* *Rev.*—Raja standing; *Kidâra* under arm.
			PRATÂPÂDITYA II., A.D. 719.
10	Æ	93	Author, common type. *Obv.*—Goddess and *Sri Pratâpa.* *Rev.*—Raja and *Kidâra* under arm.
			YAṢOVARMA, A.D. 730.[20]
11	AV	112	*Author*, common; Manikyâla Stûpa. *Goddess*, very rude; *Sri Yaṣo Varma.* *Raja*, very rude; *Kidâra* under arm.
			NAMBI OR NAMVI (?).
12	Æ	110	Author, rare. Types as preceding coins. *Obv.*—*Nambi*, with *Haka* to left. *Rev.*—*Jaya* [*De*]*va.*
			JAYA [? JAYAPIṚA], A.D. 757.
13	Æ	118	Author, unique. Types as preceding coins. *Obv.*—*Sri Jaya* . .

---

[20] This date is given on the supposition that this king is the Yaṣovarma of Kanauj who advanced to the foot of the Kashmir hills and demanded the tooth of Buddha. The only Kashmirian Yaṣovarma that I know was of the Varma family, opposed to the grandfather of Avanti Varma, the general of Ajitapiṛa, whom he defeated in A.D. 849.

PLATE IV.

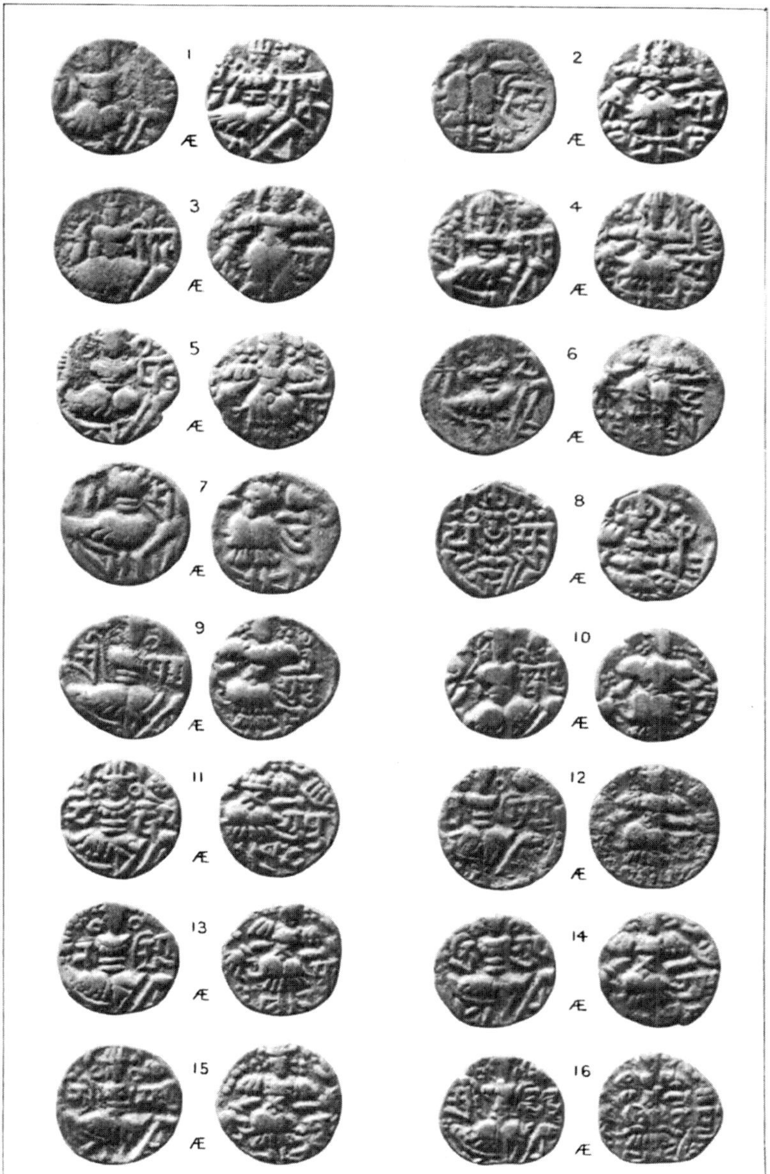

KASHMIR.

PLATE III.			JAYAPIRA OR VINAYÂDITYA, A.D. 757.
No.	Metal.	Grs.	
14	AV	120	Author, very common. *Seated Goddess ; Sri Vinayâditya.* Standing Raja ; *Jayati*, and *Kid[ara]* perpendicularly.

VARMA DYNASTY.

PLATE IV. No.	Metal.	NAMES.	OBVERSE. Seated Goddess.	REVERSE. Standing Raja.
1	Æ	Aditya Varma	*Âdi . . .*	*. . njita*
2	Æ	Sangkara Varma	*Sangkara*	*Varma*
3	Æ	Gopâla Varma	*Gopâla*	*Varma*
4	Æ	Sugandha Rânî	*Sri Sugandhâ*	*Devya*
5	Æ	Pârtha Varma	*Pârtha*	*Varma*
6	Æ	Chakra Varma	*Cha . .*	*(Va)rma Deva*
7	Æ	Unmatti Varma	*Sri*	*Unma[ti]*
		MIXED DYNASTY.		
8	Æ	Yasaskara	*Yâskara*	*Deva*
9	Æ	Parvva Gupta	*Sri Parvva*	*Gupta*
10	Æ	Kshema Gupta	*Kshema Gu-*	*-pta De-[va]*
11	Æ	Diddâkshema Gupta [21]	*Di Kshema Gu-*	*-pta*
12	Æ	Abhimanyu Gupta	*Abhimanyu*	*Gupta*
13	Æ	Nandi Gupta	*Nandi Gu-*	*-pta*
14	Æ	Tribhuvana Gupta	*Tribhuvana*	*Gupta*
15	Æ	Bhima Gupta	*Bhima Gu-*	*-pta*
16	Æ	Diddâ Rânî	*Sri Diddâ*	*Devya*

[21] Kshema Gupta, shortly after his accession, married Diddâ, with whom he was so infatuated that he added her name to his own, and called himself *Didda Kshema*, which is contracted on the coins to *Di-Kshema*. The coins with this name are extremely common, but the single-name coin is unique.

Mixed Dynasty—*continued.*

PLATE V. No.	PLATE V. Metal.	NAMES.	OBVERSE. Seated Goddess.	REVERSE. Standing Raja.
17	Æ	Sangrâma Deva	*Sangrâma Ra-*	*-ja Deva*
18	Æ	Ananta Deva	*Ananta Ra-*	*-ja Deva*
19	Æ	Kalasa	*Kalasa Ra-*	*-ja Deva*
20	BIL	Ditto	*Kalasa*	*Prama . . .*
21	AV	Harsha, 73 grains	Horseman with lance to r. *Harsha Deva*	Goddess seated
22	AV	Ditto, 72 grains	Elephant to right	*Sri Harsha Deva*
23	AR	Ditto, 23·5 grains	Same as 22	*Sri Harsha Deva*
24	Æ	Ditto	*Harsha Raja*	*Deva*
25	Æ	Uchchala	*Uchchala*	*Deva*
26	Æ	Sussala	*Sri Sussala* Some coins are without the *Sri*	*Deva*
27	Æ	Salla	*Salla Ra[ja]*	*Deva*
28	Æ	Jaya Sinha Deva I.	*Sri Jaya Sinha* Some coins have *Jaya Sinha Raja Deva*	*Deva*
29	Æ	Jaya Sinha Deva II.	*Sri Vijaya Suta*	*Sinha Deva*
29A	Æ	Sri Jaya Siratna Deva		
30	Æ	Paramânak	*Sri Para [mânaka]*	*Deva*
31	Æ	Avanti Deva	*Avanti*	*Deva*
32	Æ	Jaga Deva	*Jaga*	*Deva*
33	Æ	Raja Deva	*Sri Raja*	*Deva*
The two following coins are of the Kashmir types, but the names of the Rajas are not in any of the lists.				
34	Æ	Pratâpa Deva	*Pratâpa*	*Deva*
35	Æ	Gulhana	*Sri Gulhana*	

VI.—Rajputana and N.-W. India.

The Saka satraps of W. India [Surashtra and Mâlwa] were subdued by the Guptas about A.D. 400. The Balharas, of whom we have only some unread coins of silver, were most probably also tributary to the Guptas until Balabhi was sacked in A.D. 524 by the White Huns. As this date falls in the middle of the reign of Mihirkul,

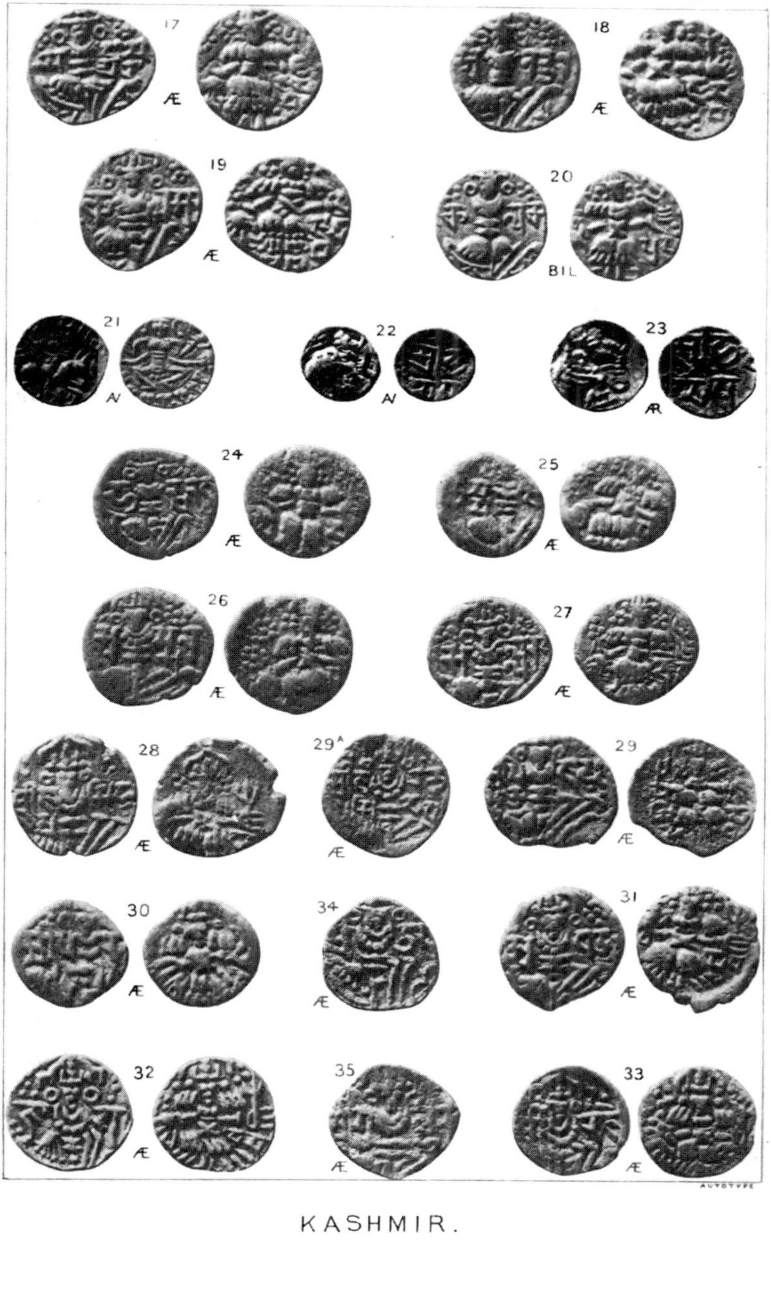

KASHMIR.

I conclude that the destruction of the city was the work of the great Ephthalite invader. His father Toramâna, the leader of the *Jâbuli* White Huns, had already conquered Sindh in A.D. 505, and W. Mâlwa about A.D. 510, in the time of Bhânu-Gupta, whose inscription at Eran is dated in S. 191 of the Gupta era, or A.D. 509. The coins of the *Jâbuli* kings of Sindh are thin broad pieces of silver, copied from the Sassanian money. They are described in my account of the White Huns, which was read before the last meeting of the Oriental Congress in 1892.

Mihirkul himself was defeated by the combined armies of the Hindu Princes of Upper India, and driven out of Rajputâna about A.D. 530.

The Indian coins of Mediæval Age, from A.D. 600 to 1200, that are found in Râjputâna and N. India, from the Sutlej eastward as far as Benares, and from the Himalaya southward to the Narbada River, consist of three distinct classes chiefly of silver, or of copper plated or only washed with silver. There is only one gold coin, Pl. VI. 18, with mediæval letters.

I. Thick pieces of silver, weighing upwards of 60 grains [Pl. VI. fig. 7], with a head on one side and an altar, or throne, on the other. These are found most plentifully in S.-W. Rajputana, in Baroda and the neighbouring districts of Mewar, Mâlwa, and Gujarât. They are known by the names of *Gadiya*, derived, as I conjecture, from the fire altar or *throne* (*gadi*) on the reverse. By the early Muhammadan writers they are described as *Tâtariya* dirhems, or as Masudi[22] writes the name *Talato-wiya* dirhems, weighing $1\frac{1}{3}$ dirhem, or $48 + 16 = 64$ grains.

[22] Sprenger's Masudi.

In weight they correspond exactly with the Greek *drachma*, and in type they are the direct descendants of the *hemi-drachms* of the Saka satraps of Surashtra and Malwa, with the *gadi*, or "throne," in place of the original *chaitya*. Even the *sun* and *moon* symbols of the Sassanian coins are retained with the fire altar or throne.

II. Thin broad pieces of silver, weighing upwards of 60 grains [Pl. VI. figs. 13—15], with a head on one side, and a fire altar with two attendant priests on the reverse. These are simply rude copies of the Sassanian coins. They are common in the Gangetic Doub, but are found more plentifully in Mewâr and Mârwâr, and throughout all Rajputâna. The early coins are without letters, but they still retain the sun and moon symbols of their Sassanian prototypes. The king's head has a beard and a moustache as on the Sassanian coins. The flames of the altar have become a mere pyramid of dots, and the attendant priests are scarcely recognisable as intended for human beings. On the later coins the title of *Sri* appears either above or behind the head, and other letters in front of the face, as *Ha*, or *Ja*, and others. It is *possible* that *Ha* may be the initial syllable of *Harsha* Vardhana's name; but this is only a guess. As the letters belong to the seventh or eighth century this tentative guess is at least plausible.

There is a large number of copper coins [Pl. VI. 1—6] which show Siva and his bull on one side, and on the reverse a very rude representation of what appears to be a fire altar with its two attendant priests. Many of them bear single letters or names in early mediæval letters. One has the name of *Rudra*, and a second has the syllable *Tri*, which may be the first syllable of a well-known name of *Siva*, either as *Trilochan*, "the three-eyed," or

Tripurântaka, "the destroyer of the Asur Tripura." The Bull Nandi and the Trident are well-known symbols of Siva. A large find of these coins was made at Rohtak, between the Sutlej and Delhi, ten years ago. They probably formed the common copper currency of the Panjab and Rajputâna between A.D. 500 and 800.

There are also smaller silver and copper coins of Sassanian types with the name of *Sri Somala Deva* [Pl. VI., 10—12), of whom we know nothing. As the copper coins bear a horseman they were probably copied from the coins of the Brahmani kings of Kabul, and would therefore date in the ninth or tenth century A.D.

Another class of silver coins of Sassanian type bears the name of *Sri Vigraha* (Pl. VI. 16), while some have *Sri Ja.*

The latest class of these coins is quite different. On the obverse is the figure of the Varâha incarnation of Vishnu, and on the reverse, in letters of the ninth century, the legend *Srimad Adi Varâha*, which was the title borne by Bhoja Deva of Kanauj in A.D. 850—900.

All these coins were known by the general name of *drammas* or *dramyas*, of which several distinct kinds are mentioned in the *Siṛon* (or *Siḍoniya*) inscription, with dates from A.D. 903 to 968.[23] The following kinds, I believe, may be identified with some of the specimens in Pl. VI. I will describe these separately under the letters A, B, C, and D.

A.—*Drammas*, without any special name.
B.—*Srimad Ádi Varâha drammas.*
C.—*Vigraha Pâla drammas.*
D.—*Panchiyaka drammas.*

---

[23] *Epigraphia Indica*, i., 167.

Drammas, or *Dramyas*, are also mentioned in the following inscriptions:—

Gwalior—A.D. 875, 876. *Srimad Adi Varâha*; title of Bhoja Deva of Mahodaya or Kanauj.[24]
Pehewa—A.D. 903-907. Mahendra Pâla Deva—*Dharmas*.[25]
Asni—A.D. 917. Mahi Pâla Deva—*Dra.* 500.[26]
Jaunpur—A.D. 1216. 2,250 *Shad-Boddika Drammas*.[27]
Besâni—A.D. 1207. *Dra.* 10; *Dra.* 1,000.[28]

The simple Drammas, A, I take to be the small thick pieces of silver (Pl. VI., 7), weighing upwards of 60 grains, or up to 65 and 66 full weight, which are generally known in Gujarât and Mâlwa as *Gadiya* coins, and also as *Chaukaduka*. There is a weight called *gadyânak* of 36 *ratis*, or 65·5 grains at 1·82 grains to the rati, but the weight varies very much according to the value of the rati. I take the common dramma to be the lineal descendant of the Greek drachm of 67·2 grains full weight, and I would identify it with the *Shad-boddika dramma* of the Jaunpur inscription. The *vodri* or *boddika* was the name of the ¼ pana, or *pâdika* of silver = 11·2 grains, or exactly the same as the Greek *obolus*.

The *Srimad Adi Varâha Dramma*, B (Pl. VI., figs. 20, 21), was of the same weight as A, ranging up to 63 grains.

The *Vigraha Pâla*, C, was also of the same weight as A (Pl. VI., 16). Fractions of this coin are also mentioned

---

[24] The Gwalior inscription of the rock-cut Temple states that the Governor of Gopâdri was appointed by King *Srimad Adi Varâha*, or Raja Bhoja Deva.

[25] *Epigraphia Indica*, i., 184-185.

[26] *Indian Antiquary*, xvi., 174.

[27] *Archæol. Survey*, xi., 176.

[28] *Archæol. Survey*, xxi., 102.

as ⅓ and ⅓ of a Vigraha Pâla dramma, but as no small coins of this type have been found, the fraction must have been in copper coins.

The *Panchiyaka-dramma*, D, I understand to have been a piece of "five boddikas," as its name seems to imply. Its full weight would therefore have been five times 11·2 grains, or 56 grains. This weight answers exactly to that of the silver coins of the Kabuli Brahman coins, twelve of which in my cabinet average 54 grains.

With the single exception of the *Adi Varâha* coins, none of the pieces represented in Plate VI. have yet been assigned to any known kings. We know nothing of any prince named *Somala Deva* (Figs. 10, 11, 12), and we cannot fix the country of *Vigraha*. As the *Siṛon* inscription calls the coins *Vigraha Pâla drammas*, the prince may have belonged to the Raghuvansa family of Bhoja Deva, as all of his known successors took the suffix of Pâla, as in the following list, according to the *Pehewa*, *Siṛon*, and *Asni* inscriptions.

Probable Accession. A.D.		Dates. A.D.
860	BHOJA-DEVA . . .	862, 875, 882
885	Mahendra Pâla Deva . .	903—907
910	Kshiti Pâla, or Mahi Pala .	917—918
935	Deva Pâla . . .	948

The only Vigraha Pâlas that I know belong to the Pala Rajas of Magadha. Their dates would suit, but we have not hitherto found any of their coins. The following names precede that of *Mahipâla*, who certainly possessed Benares, and whose date is well ascertained.

Accession. A.D.		
910	Vigraha Pâla I.	
925	Nârâyana Pâla	
950	Rajya Pâla	
965	Râma Pâla	
980	Vigraha Pâla II.	S. 12 of reign
1015	Mahi Pâla	V.S. 1083=A.D. 1026

During some excavations of the ruins of the Vajrâsan Vihâra at *Ghosrâwa* in Magadha I found some silver coins of Vigraha, one of which differed from the usual type in having no king's head, the inside of the obverse being occupied with the name in large letters *Sri Vi* (*graha*), see Plate VI., fig. 17.[29]

RAJPUTÂNA AND W. INDIA.

PLATE VI. No.	Metal.	Grs.	
1	Æ		British Museum. *Prinsep's Antiquities*, by E. Thomas. [Pl. XXXIV. 17, 18.] *King to front*, with spear in left hand. *Sun*. Indian legend, *Ghuta*, or *Shuta*.
2	Æ		British Museum. *Prinsep's Antiquities*, by E. Thomas. [Pl. XXXIV. 12.] *Siva and his Bull Nandi*, as on the coins of Vasu Deva. *Fire Altar* (?) Indian legend, *Rudra*.
	Æ		*Prinsep's Antiquities*, by E. Thomas. [Pl. XXXIV. 11.] *Siva and Bull*. *Rev.*—Trident with *Tri*.
3	Æ		Author, four specimens from large find at Rohtak. *Siva and Bull*. *Rev.*—Rude Fire Altar; attendant to left; *Bal* in monogram to right.

[29] *Archæol. Survey of India*, xi., 175, and Plate XLIII.

PLATE VI.

RAJPUTANA AND N. W. INDIA.

PLATE VI.

No.	Metal.	Grs.	
4	Æ		British Museum. *Siva and Bull. Rev.*—Rude Fire Altar; attendant to right; wheel to left.
5	Æ		*Siva and Bull. Rev.*—Rude Fire Altar; Trident to right.
6	Æ		*Siva and Bull. Rev.*—Rude Fire Altar, with an attendant on each side.
7	Ꞧ	65	From *Baroda* and *Malwâ*; common; called *Gadia*. *Rude Head of King* to right, with numerous dots and other indescribable marks. Rude Fire Altar or Throne (*Gadi*), with symbols of Sun and Moon.
8	Æ	66	Similar types as on No. 7; common; in Mâlwa, Gujarat, and Rajputâna.
9	Æ		*Prinsep's Antiquities*, by E. Thomas. [Pl. XXVII. 19.] *Obv.—Hâsa* or *Hânsa*, with *S. ho* below. *Rev.—Sri*, with ornamental lines and dots.
10	Ꞧ	65	Author, Rajputâna; unique. Rude head to right. *Rev.—Sri Somala De[va]*.
11	Æ	33	Author, Rajputâna; in 3 sizes of 65, 33 and 17 grains. Rude Horseman to right; copied from Kabul Brahmani coins. *Rev.—Sri Somala Deva*
12	Æ	29	Author, Rajputâna; unique. Horseman galloping to left. *Sri Somala Deva.*
13	Ꞧ		Dr. Hoërnle, from Marwâr, British Museum. *Rude Head of King* to right; copied from Sassanian coins. *Rev.—Rude copy of Fire Altar* and two attendants, with symbols of Sun and Moon.
14	Ꞧ	57	Author, duplicate Mr. Theobald; Rajputâna; common. See E. Thomas. [Pl. XXXIII. 7, 8.]

PLATE VI. No.	Metal.	Grs.	
			Rude Head of King to right; Indian *Sri* over head, and *Ha* before face, perhaps for *Harsha*. *Rev.*—Rude Fire Altar with two attendants.
15	Æ	65	Mr. Theobald; a plated coin. *Rude Head of King* to right; before face, Indian *Sri Va* (one letter lost). *Rev.*—*Rude Fire Altar*, with two attendants.
16	Æ	62	Author; duplicate Mr. Theobald; common, but seldom good. Rude Head of King to right; before face, *Sri*; below, *Vigra(ha.)* *Rev.*—Indian letter M in middle in place of Fire Altar. One attendant on each side.
17	Æ		Author, found in the ruins of Monastery at Ghosrâwa, in Magadha (*Archæ. Survey*, xi. Pl. XLIII. 1, 2.) Legend in middle of obverse instead of King's head; *Sri Vi* [*graha.*] *Rev.*—Fire Altar with two attendant priests.
18	AV	13·5	Author. Obverse, *Sri*. Reverse, *Sivaye*.
19	Æ		Mr. Theobald, and a duplicate. Head with the letter *Ja* in front of face. ,Rude Fire Altar with attendants.
20	Æ	62	Author, common in Rajputâna and N. India. Figure of the *Varâha Avatâr* of Vishnu to right with left leg raised; below, a small lion; to right, a sun symbol; behind, a trident. *Rev.*—Legend in 2 lines; *Srimad Âdi Varâha*, with traces of two attendants to right and left, and remains of Fire Altar below.
21	Æ		The Âdi Varâha coins completed from several examples. The coins are usually very small and imperfect.
22	Æ	16	Author, very thin, light coin. Horseman to right. Prostrate man lying on his stomach; above, *Sri Tri-vi*.

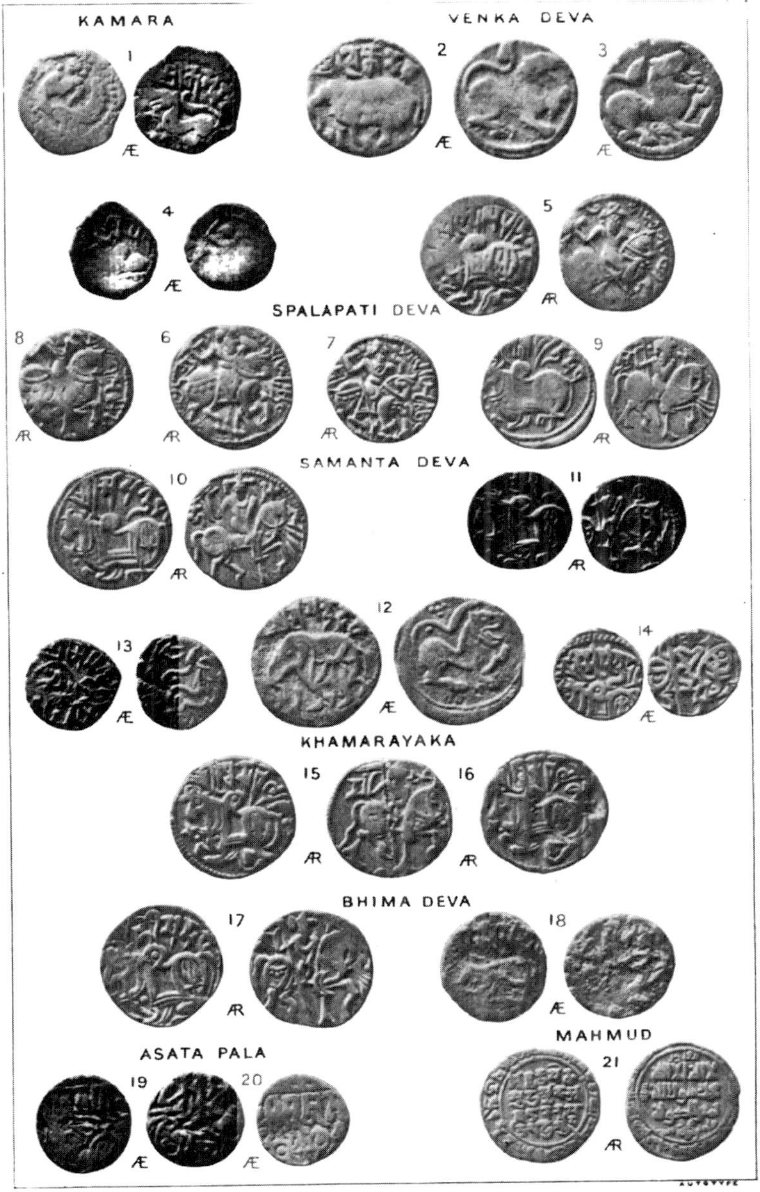

GANDHARA AND PANJAB.

PLATE VI. No.	Metal.	Grs.	
23	Æ	19	Author, very thin light coin; apparently double struck. Horseman to right; a second horseman appears behind. Prostrate man lying on his stomach; above, *Sri Tri-vi.* The legend on these coins is probably intended for *Sri Trivikrama*, a well-known title of Vishnu, referring to the three steps or paces which he made in the "*Dwarf Avatâra.*"

VII.—Gandhâra and Panjab.

The main source of our knowledge of the Brahman kings of Kabul is *Alberuni*, who came to India with Mahmud only a century after their rule had come to an end. Some additional information can be gleaned from his copyists, and still more from the numerous coins of the kings, which are still found in great numbers in the Kabul valley, in the Punjab, and all over North India. After mentioning the great Kushân king, Kanik (or Kanishka), who built the *Vihâra* of Purushâwar, he adds, "The last king of this race was *Al Kitormân*,[30] and his Vazir was *Kallar*, a Brahman." The latter had been fortunate in finding a hidden treasure, which gave him much influence and power. The Vazir imprisoned the Raja and seized the throne. "After him ruled the Brahman kings, *Sâmand, Kamalu, Bhîm, Jaipâl, Anandpâl, Tarojanpâl.* The latter was killed A.H. 412 (A.D. 1021), and his son *Bhîmpâl* five years later (A.D. 1026)."

[30] M. Sachau, ii., p. 13, gives the name as *Lagaturmân*; but E. Thomas has shown that both Arabic and Persian copies which he consulted read *Kitormân.*

In this account it will be observed that the early kings are called *Deva*, while all the last four kings are called *Pâla.* Now it is remarkable that while we have coins of the first four kings, we have not found even a single specimen of any one of the last four. My inference is that these last four princes were of a different family. They are in fact always called *Shâhi* by *Alberuni* himself, as well as by others. Their territories extended "from Kashmir to Multan and from Sarhind to Lamghan ;" [31] and we learn from Masudi (who died A.H. 345 = A.D. 956) that the king of Kandahar (Gandhâra) is called *Hahaj*, which name is common to all sovereigns of that country ; [32] and he further adds that Kandahar is called the country of the *Rajput.* I conclude, therefore, that *Jaipâl*, who was the contemporary of Masudi, must have been a Rajput, and not a Brahman ; and further, that he may have been a *Janjuha* (Jajah) Rajput, which tribe was at that very time in possession of the hill country between the Indus and Jhelam. According to Ferishta, also, *Jaipâl* was the son of *Ishtpal* (or *Asatpal*).

Alberuni further says that "this Hindu *Shâhi* dynasty is now extinct (after the deaths of Trilochan Pâl and Bhim Pâl)," and that "the pedigree of this royal family written on silk exists in the fortress Nagarkot (Kangra), which belonged to Trilochanpâl." I conclude, therefore, that after the death of the *Brahman* king Bhimpâl, the Rajput *Jaypâl*, son of *Asatpâl*, had regained the throne of his ancestors, the *Shâhiya dynasty.* I note that *Anandpâl* is called *Shâhi* by Alberuni (i. 136), and that *Trilochan Pal*, the opponent of Mahmud, is always spoken of as "*the Shâhi*" in the *Raja Tarangini.* I think that I can

---

[31] Briggs's *Ferishta*, i. 15. [32] H. M. Elliot, i. 22.

trace this family a few generations farther back by their title of *Shâhi*, as I make a guess that they may have belonged to the dynasty of Little Kushâns, or *Shâh Kitors*, who were driven out by the Brahman Kallar. Thus I find in the *Raja Tarangini* a chief named *Lalliya Shâhi* was deposed by Gopâla Varma of Kashmir about A.D. 902, who set up his son *Tomarâna Shâhi* in his father's place. If we place *Asatpâl*, the father of Jaypâl, in A.D. 925, Jaypâl himself will succeed naturally about 950 A.D. The enthronement of *Jaipâl* would thus have been a simple restoration of the *Little Kushâns* or *Shâh Kitors* to their old kingdom.

There is some difficulty in arranging the dates of these two lines of kings, the *Brahmans* and the *Shâhis*. The following facts are our only guides :—

I.—*Kanik*, the last of the Kitorman kings, was dethroned by his Vazir, the Brahman Kallar; but after some time *Kanik* regained his throne.

II.—After Kanik's death the Brahman Sâmand became king.

III.—*Yakub Soffâri*, A.D. 873—878, took Kabul, and struck coins at Panjshir, in A.H. 260-261, A.D. 873—874.

IV.—*Amru Soffâri*, A.D. 878—900, took *Kamalu* (or Kalmu) prisoner. [H. M. Elliot, ii. 423, from Jâmi al Hikâyât.]

The author was a gossiping story-teller, who wrote as late as the thirteenth century. I doubt his accuracy, and prefer the authority of Alberuni, who was in India early in the eleventh century.

V.—Silver coin of bull and horseman type, Al Muktadir Billah A.D. 907—932; outline figure.

VI.—Copper coin of Al Mutaki Billah A.D. 940—944; outline figures.

VII.—Masudi, about A.H. 332=A.D. 943, died A.D. 956, calls the king a Rajput.

There is a difficulty also about the names of some of the kings, which ought to agree with those of the coins.

A.—Alberuni calls the king the last of the Kitorman rulers, who was dethroned by his Brahman minister, *Kanik*, whom E. Thomas and Sir Clive Bayley identify with *Sri Varka* of the coins (Pl. VII. fig. 2). I read the name as *Venka*, because the letter *reph* or *r* is always placed *above the line* of mâtras, whereas in the present case the letter combined with the *K* is on the same line as the *mâtras*. The vowel *e* of the initial letter *V* is distinct on all my coins.

B.—*Kallar*, the name of the Brahman Vazir, is identified with the Spalapati of the coins. Prinsep, Thomas, and Bayley have uniformly read this name as *Syâlapati*, but their reading is certainly wrong, as the letter attached to the initial *S* is *P* and not *Y*, and consequently the true name is *Spalapati*, which was the actual title of the *war minister* in Persia, Parthia, Hyrkania, and Armenia. I therefore take *Kallar* (probably *Kalas* or *Kalhan*) to have been the name, and *Spalapati* the designation by which he was usually known. In Persian and Armenian the military commanders are usually spoken of by this title, and not by their actual names. The title is not foreign to India, as it is only the Sanskrit *Samara-pati*, or "war-lord," that is, the "commander-in-chief." In Persia the "war-minister" of Kobâd, named Sufrai, was put to death by Sapor by order of the king, who installed Sapor as *Sparapet*, or *Sipehbed*, in his stead.[33] Hormazd IV. was the son of the daughter of the Asparapati, a Parthian chief.[34] The maternal uncle of Khosroes I. was the *Aspabed* or *Sparabed*, which Elisæus explains as a "military chief."[35]

---

[33] Geo. Rawlinson, Seventh Monarchy.
[34] Patkanian.
[35] Elisæus, p. 8, and 11, note 4.

C.—The name of *Kamalu* or *Kamlua* has not yet been found on any coin. But there is one coin name, read by E. Thomas as *Khwadava* (Pl. VII. figs. 15 and 16), and by Bayley as *Khvadavayakah,* which most numismatists consider as the representative of *Kamalu.* I read this name differently as *Khamaradaka* or *Khamarayaka,* with which the Arabic قملو may be made to correspond by slight change to قملکي, or *Kamalaka,* the one name having *r* where the other has *l.*

The following list of these Brahman and Rajput kings of Kabul and the Panjab is tentative, as we have very few precise dates to guide us. The accession of the Brahman Kallar has been variously assigned, but I believe that it may be fixed very closely by the fact, noted by Ibn Khallikan,[36] that in the time of Yakub Soffâri Kabul was held by Turks of the *Darâri* tribe. No tribe of this name is known; but it is certain that they were not *Brahmans.* If for دراري we might read کداري or *Kidâri,* we could then assign the throne of Kabul to a prince of the *Little Kushâns,* or descendants of *Kidâr,* who were certainly Turks. This prince would have been *Venka* of the coins, who was dethroned by his minister, the Brahman *Kallar.* But eventually Venka regained his throne, according to the three different authorities quoted by E. Thomas,[37] and not until his death did the Brahman Sâmand get possession of the throne.

How the Rajput Jaypâl, the *Shâhi,* gained the kingdom is not mentioned by Alberuni. But the change of name from the simple *Deva* of the Brahman kings to the *Pâla Deva* of their four successors, and the mysterious

---

[36] H. M. Elliot, ii. 413.

[37] *Hindu Kings of Kabul,* pp. 194, 195.

absence of any coins of the Shâhis would seem to show some great revolution. Ferishta calls Jaypâl the son of *Ishtpâl,* who may perhaps be the *Asat Pâl* of some rare coins of the Bull and Horseman type, which I have given in Plate VII., figs. 19—20. I hazard a guess that Asatpal may have been a son of *Tomarâna* Shâhi, and the grandson of Lâlliya Shâhi, of whom the author of the *Raja Tarangini* says that he was "among kings even as the sun is among stars."

I have placed the probable accession of *Jaypâl* as early as 950 A.D. because I find that the Shâhi of Kabul had a grown-up son, between 964 and 973, who accompanied the rebel *Lawik,* and was defeated by Sabuktigin at Charkh, in the Lohgarh Valley, between Kabul and Ghazni. But the Shâhi king is mentioned at a still earlier date in the *Raja Tarangini,* in which it is stated that *Diddâ Râni's* mother was a Shâhi princess (vi. 177). Now Diddâ Râni became the Queen of Kshema Gupta not later than A.D. 951; and if we place her birth not later than A.D. 935, and her mother's birth not later than 920 A.D., her grandfather, the *Shâhi King,* must be placed at least as early as A.D. 920, during the time of the Brahman king *Sâmanta Deva.* But though the line of Shâhi princes still adhered to their ancient title, their former power was not recovered until the time of Jaypâl. This is distinctly shown by the *Jhûsi* copper plate inscription of Trilochan Pâl, which recounts his genealogy from *Vijaya Pâla,* omitting all earlier ancestors.[38] The title of Shâhi is not given, but all three kings take the high-sounding titles of

Parama Bhattâraka, Mahârâjâdhirâja, Parameswara.

---

[38] *Indian Antiquary,* xviii. 34.

Jayapâl probably at first held Kabul, but in 977 A.D. he encountered Sabuktigin at Lamghân, and in A.D. 1000 he fought with Mahmud near Peshâwar, or more correctly near his capital of *Wehand,* now called Ohind, on the Indus above Attak. He died a voluntary death in 1002, and was succeeded by his son, Anand Pâl, who was defeated by Mahmud in 1008 A.D. As the Muhammadans advanced the Indians retired. At first they occupied *Bhîra,* on the Jhelam, but being driven out in 1004, they retired to the northern mountains. Trilochan Pâl succeeded in A.D. 1014, and in 1018 he was defeated by Mahmud on the banks of the Taushi or Tohi River (*Raja Tarangini,* vii., 55). Troyer, in his translation, reads *Taushi* as the name of the month in which the battle was fought, but as there are no less than three streams of this name in the North Punjab—first near Punach, second near Rajaori, third near Jammu—I accept the native translator's opinion that it is a river. Trilochan retired after his defeat to Hastikâm (*Raja Tarangini,* vii., 65). He continued to retreat to India and was again defeated by Mahmud on the banks of the *Ráhib.* His son Bhimpâl was betrothed to the daughter of Chand Rai of *Sharwa,* "one of the greatest men in Hind" according to Utbi.[39] Here we lose sight of him; but the Jhusi inscription informs us that he was still alive in A.D. 1027.

The royal family of the Shâhis continued to flourish for several hundred years, and gave many queens to Kashmir. The two Queens of Harsha, A.D. 1089—1100, were Shâhi princesses.

---

39 H. M. Elliot, ii. 47.

Brâhmans and Râjput Shâhis.

A.D.	Brâhmans.	A.D.	Shâhis.
860	Venka	870	Lalliya Shâhi
870	. . Yakub Soffâri conquers Kabul		
873	. . strikes coins at Panjshir		
875	*Kallar*, Brahman, or *Spalapati Deva*	883	Lalliya Shâhi, dethroned by Sangkara Varma
895	Venka restored		
900	*Sâmanta Deva*	902	Tomarâna Shâhi, placed on throne by Gopâla Varma
		930	Isht-pâl (Aṣatpâl), recorded father of
940	*Kamlua*		
945	*Bhîma Deva*		
	Rajputs.		
950	Jay Pâl, Shâhi. 964—973. His son defeated by Sabuktigin		Vijaya Pâla Deva (Jhusi Copper Plate)
1002	Anand Pâl Shâhi		Ananda Pâla Deva
1012	Trilochan Pâl Shahi		Trilochana Pâla Deva
1021	Bhîm Pâl Shâhi		
1026	Recorded end of Shâhiya dynasty	1027	Trilochan—still alive V.S. 1084 = A.D. 1027

GANDHARA AND PANJAB.

PLATE VII. No.	Metal.	Grs.	
			Kamara.
1	Æ	30·3	British Museum. *Sir Clive Bayley*; (*Num. Chron.*, 1882) an early coin; before *Venka Deva* (?) 850 A.D.
			Peacock with outspread wings to left.
			Lion to left; *Indian Legend, Sri Kamara.*
			Venka-Deva, A.D. 860.
2	Æ	52	Author; also of middle size, 42 grains; and of small size, 18 grains.

PLATE VII. No.	Metal.	Grs.	
3	Æ		*Elephant* walking to left. Legend, *Sri Venka Deva.* *Lion* to right, tail over back. N.B —Single letters are found on some coins below the Lion, as D, Pi, R, V.
			VENKA-DEVA—RESTORED (?) A.D. 895.
4	Æ	19	*Author*, unique. *Humped Bull*, Sri Ve . . . *Horseman.* N.B.—As these are the types of Spalapati's coins, I venture to assign the coin to the second reign of Venka Deva.
			SPALAPATI DEVA, A.D. 875.
5	AR	54	*Author.* *Recumbent humped Bull* to left, with *trisul* of Siva on flank, and ornamental cloth covering over body. Legend, *Sri Spalapati Deva.* *Horseman* to right, with long lance in right hand, and left hand before face, holding some indistinct object. *Legend in unknown characters to right.* Single Indian letters occur on the reverse to the upper left, as A, Gu, K; perhaps the initials of Mint cities.
6 7 8 9	AR AR AR AR		Author. These specimens present various readings of the unknown legends on the reverse. Nos. 8 and 9 seem to be of rather later date, the figures approaching the outline representations like those of the coins of the later kings.
			I reject all the readings of dates, as proposed by E. Thomas and Clive Bayley. There are two distinctly different legends, neither of which has yet been read. One is shown on Figs. 5, 6, 7; the other on Fig. 8. Fig. 9 is the same as that in Sâmanta Deva's coins.
—	Æ		All the copper coins of Spalapati are of the same type as his silver coins. They are of the same size, and were apparently struck from the same dies.

PLATE VII.

No.	Metal.	Grs.	
			Sâmanta Deva, a.d. 900.
10	AR	50	*Author*, very common. Six good coins, average 50 grains. *Recumbent humped Bull* in outline to left. Legend, *Sri Sâmanta Deva.* Horseman to right, with long lance in right hand, and left hand raised before face, holding some indistinct object. Three letters or figures to right. To left, the Indian letter *Bhi*, perhaps for Bhira.
11	AR	33	*Author.* Coin of small size; rare. Only six specimens, average 33·3 grains. *Recumbent humped Bull* to left, with *trisul* of Siva on flank, *Sri Sâmanta Deva.* Horseman to right with long lance. Plume on horse's head. Three letters or figures to right. N.B.—These coins are smaller and their types are also smaller than No. 10.
12	Æ	40	*Author*, common
13	Æ	12	*Author*, common
—	Æ	5·1	*Author*, common
			(Nos. 12, 13, —) Types of elephant and lion, as on Venka Deva's coins. Coins of three sizes, weighing about 42, 14, and 7 grains.
14	Æ	52	Author, very common in Punjab and N. India. Thick coins. Recumbent Bull and Horseman types, *Sri Sâmanta Deva.*
			Khamarayaka. (?) Kamalua, a.d. 940.
15	AR	46	*Author.* Rare; average of seven coins, 46 grains. (Nos. 15, 16) *Recumbent humped Bull* to left; *Sri Khamarayakah.* Horseman with lance to right. Three letters or figures to right; unread. In field to left, on different coins, the single letters A, K, Bhi, M.
16	AR	46	
			Bhîma-Deva, a.d. 945.
17	AR	50	*Author*, very rare *Recumbent humped Bull* to left. *Sri Bhîma Deva.*

PLATE VII. No.	Metal.	Grs.	
			Horseman to right with lance. Three unknown letters or figures to right. To left, the single letter N.
18	Æ	24	Author, unique.
			Elephant to left. *Sri Bhima Deva.*
			Lion to right, as on coins of *Venka* and Sâmanta.
			Aṣata-Pala.
19	Æ	48	*Author*, very rare. Only five specimens.
			Recumbent humped Bull to left. *Sri Aṣata Pâla.*
			Horseman to right.
20	Æ	48	Similar types; but legend, *Sri Aṣata .. ra.*

No coins have yet been found of the *Shâhi Kings* Jayapâla, Ananda Pâla, and *Trilochana* Pâla; but the Bull and Horseman types were continued by the Ghaznivide conquerors, of whom a specimen may be seen in Sir Clive Bayley's Plate, fig. 22, with the name of *Masaud* above the horseman, and the name of *Sri Sâmanta Deva* above the Bull on the other side. I possess other coins of the same kind of Modud and Ferokhzâd. But the most interesting coins of the transition period are the dirhems of Mahmûd himself, which were struck at Lahor, with a translation of the Muhammadan Kalimeh in Sanskrit. A specimen of this coin was first made known by E. Thomas. I have possessed only four specimens of this rare coin, one of which I will now describe.

Mahmud of Ghazni, a.d. 1027.

No.	Metal.	Grs.			
21	Æ	45	Sanskrit legend in middle of coin.	*Abyaktam eka Muhammad A vatára Nripa ti Mahmud.*	The one Eternal: Muhammad the Messenger: King Mahmud.

Circular legend, *Ayam tankam Mahmudpur ghatite Hijriyena Samvati* 418. "This

PLATE VII. No.	Metal.	Grs.	
			tanka (was struck) at Mahmudpur in the Hijra year 418 (= A.D. 1027.) E. Thomas has read the latter half of the circular legend differently, thus: *ghate tatâ jikiyera Samvati* 418. *Mahmudpur* is a correction of Alberuni's *Mandahukur*, "the capital of *Lohâwar*, E. of the River Irâwa" [Sachau I., 206].

The horseman on these coins is caparisoned after the fashion that prevailed in the East in mediæval times. I have seen numerous pictures of Eastern kings from Mahmud of Ghazni down to Muhammad Ghori, commonly known as Muhammad bin Sâm; and one of the latter king now lies before me. He is represented on horseback going to the right as on these Hindu coins, and carrying a lance in his right hand with a pennon floating from the top. His left arm is raised in front of his face, and apparently holds out a small buckle. It certainly does *not* hold the bridle rein, which is seemingly connected with the pommel of the saddle, as on the coins. It is this raised arm that on the later coins has been taken for the letter *lâm*, ل of the Arabic *adl*, عدل, the letters *ad* being actually the initial letters of the legend in unknown characters. The king wears long jack-boots, and a helmet with crest, and a back-piece covering the neck. He has also a sword fastened to his waist, and a quiver of arrows at his back. The rider's legs and the horse's flanks are protected by *chauris*, or tails of the Tibetan long-haired ox. But none of these latter equipments are found on the coins.

The types of the humped bull and horseman were at once adopted by the kings of Ghazni until their extinction, and were afterwards continued by Muhammad bin Sâm and his successors in Ghazni and Delhi down to the

PLATE VIII.

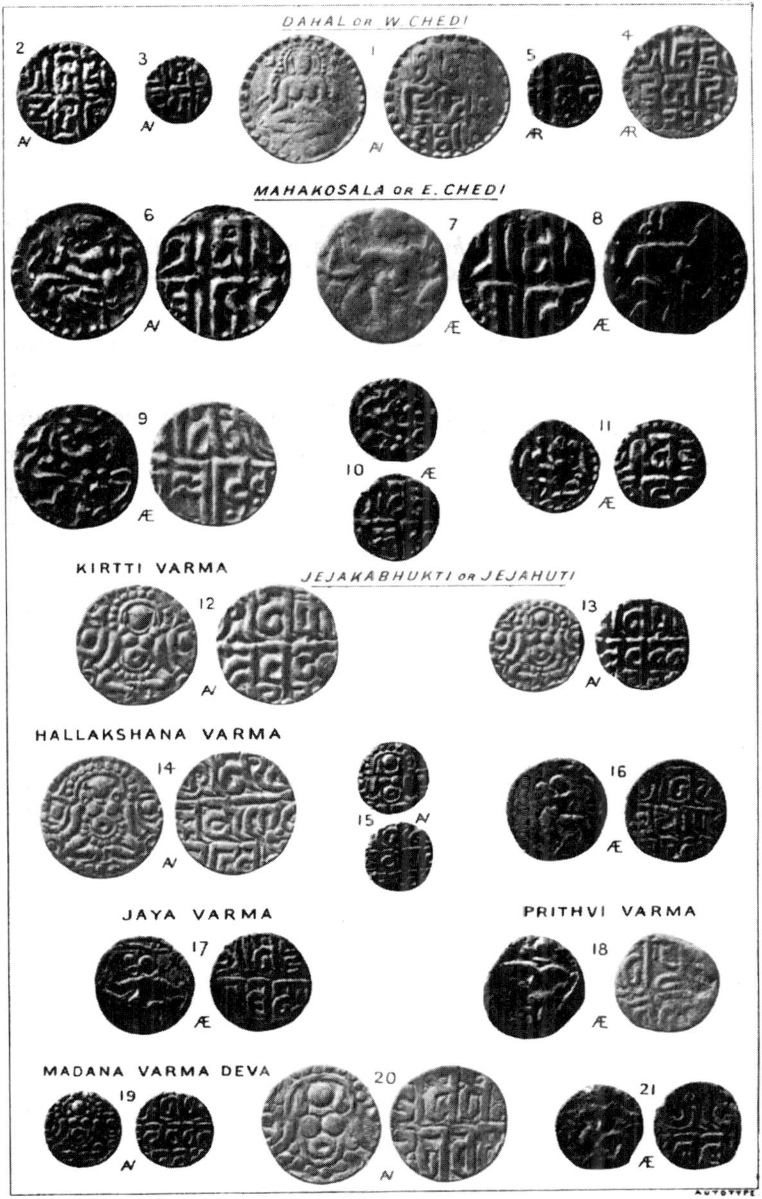

W. AND E. CHEDI — JEJAHUTI OR MAHOBA.

time of Balban, A.D. 1265, of whom I possessed a single coin with the horseman on one side. But though the type was disused at Delhi, it was continued on the coinage of the petty Rajas of Kangra down to the time of Triloka Chandra, a contemporary of Jahangir in A.D. 1620. Altogether, therefore, it continued in use for the long period of upwards of seven hundred and fifty years.

But the Indo-Scythian types of the standing Raja and the seated goddess Lakshmi, which were introduced by Kanishka in A.D. 79, lasted for a much longer period, having been continued on the coinage of Kashmir down to the Muhammadan conquest in A.D. 1339, or for twelve hundred and forty years.

VIII.—Chedis of Dahâl and Maha-Kosala.

The *Chedis*, or *Haihayas*, of Central India claimed descent from Sahasra-Arjuna, or Kârtavirya, through Haihaya, a descendant of Yadu, the progenitor of the Yâdavas. The Chedis are mentioned in the Mahâbhârata with their chief city of Manipura, which was the capital of Chitrângada, whose daughter Chitrângadâ became the mother of Babhruvâhana—by Arjuna Pândava. Manipura is popularly believed to have been in *Maha Kosala*, or *E. Chedi*, the present district of Chatisgarh and Raypur, in the Central Provinces. The province includes all the country watered by the Mahanadi River and its tributaries. But the capital of the *Haihaya* king *Kârtavirya* was Mahishmati, on the Narbadâ, in *W. Chedi*, or *Dâhal*. It apparently included all the country watered by the Upper Narbada and its tributaries.

In all the inscriptions of Mahâ Kosala the rulers are

styled *Chedi-narendra*, *Chedindra*, or *Chediswara*, or "Ruler of the Chedis."[40] But from an early date they had spread over the province of *Jejâhuti*, on the Ken and Betwa Rivers; and at a later period they occupied the country on the Tamasa, or Tons River, now known as Bâghelkhand. After their conquest of Jejâhuti, with its strong fortress of Kâlanjar, they proudly styled their rulers *Kâlanjarâdhipati*, or "lords of Kalanjar"—a title which both branches claimed in their inscriptions down to the latest times. They also founded an era of their own, called the *Chedi Samvat*, or the *Kulachuri Samvat*. As this era dates from A.D. 249, I infer that their occupation of Kâlanjar must have been the occasion on which it was founded. Both branches of the family used it down to their fall.

The kingdom of *Dâhal*, or *W. Chedi*, as known in historical times, had for its capital Tripura, now Tewar, on the Narbadâ, a few miles to the west of Jabalpur. It is mentioned by Varâha Mihira in the *Brihat Sanhita*, A.D. 550. This country, with its capital and its reigning king, are all mentioned by Alberuni.[41] "*Dahâla*," he says, "is a country the capital of which is *Tiauri* (Tripuri), and the ruler of which is now *Gangeya*." This was the king who first introduced the coins shown in Plate VIII., which were afterwards copied by the *Chandella* Rajas of Mahoba, the Rahtors of Kanauj, and even by Muhammad bin Sâm, the conqueror of Delhi. But, strange to say, not one of his successors imitated his example, and his coins in gold, silver, and copper still remain the only specimens of the money of the powerful *Chedi* kings of

---

[40] *Archæol. Survey*, xvii. 71.

[41] Sachau's Alberuni, i. 202; Reinaud *Fragments*, pp. 85—106, gives the names as Dhâl, Tipuri, and Ganges.

Dâhal. They are, however, rather numerous, and their issue may have been sufficient for the wants of the country.

At some early date a third branch of the Kulachuri clan found its way to the south to the banks of the Godâveri River, where they appear to have reigned previous to the establishment of the Chalukya kings of Kalyân.

In the Yeur inscription the Chalukyas are designated as the destroyers of the authority of the Rashtrakutas and the Kalachuryas.[42] Mangalisa Chalukya, who reigned from A.D. 530 to 550, is specially mentioned as having ravished the power of the Kalachuris like a thunderbolt. At last, in A.D. 1153, Bijjala Deva *Kalachuri*, the commander-in-chief, expelled the Chalukya Raja, Tailapa Deva, who retired to Banawâsi. Bijjala then assumed the title of *Mahârâjâdhirâja* and *Kâlanjarâdhipati*, thus proving that he belonged to the same clan as the Kalachuris of Dâhala and Mahakosala.

The dates of the inscriptions of the two northern branches is always recorded in their own era, which is called indifferently either the *Chedi Samvat* or the *Kalachuri Samvat*, which I have shown to have been established in A.D. 249. I conclude therefore, with some confidence, that their power must have been consolidated at that date. But we have no detailed lists of their kings that reach up to so early a date. There are local chronicles of the Haihaya kings of Mahakosala of Ratanpur, but I do not think that they are trustworthy until mediæval times, when they can be corroborated by existing inscriptions. But there is good evidence regarding the Rajas of *Dâhal*,

---

[42] Walter Elliot, *Royal As. Soc. Journal*, iv. 39.

or *W. Chedi* from the time of *Kokalla* I., from whom the detailed genealogy is given both in the Benares and the Bilhari inscriptions, and who is said to have warred with Bhoja Deva, a Raja of the West. I take this *Bhoja Deva* to be the king whose inscriptions have been found at Gwalior, at Deogarh, and at Pehewa, with dates A.D. 862, 875, 882. The same date may be derived from the fact that *Krishna* Raja Râshtrakuta is recorded to have married Mahâdevî, the daughter of Kokalla.[43] The date deduced for Krishna Raja is A.D. 870—890.

Of *Lakshmana Raja*, the third in descent from Kokalla, it is recorded that his daughter Vouta Devi married the Chalukya king Vikramaditya IV., who died in A.D. 973.

Of Kokalla II., we learn that he was a great warrior, which is confirmed by the fact that there is an inscription bearing his name at *Khajurâho*, one of the great cities of the Chandellas.

Of Gânggeya Deva, I have already quoted Alberuni's statement that he was the reigning king of Dâhal in A.D. 1030.

Of *Karna Deva* and his successors we have no coins, but there are inscriptions of all of them down to the close of the dynasty by the conquests of the Baghela Rajputs and the Gonds at the end of the twelfth century A.D. Of Karna Deva himself, we have a fine copper-plate inscription dated in the year 793 of the Chedi Samvat in the second year of his reign, or A.D. 1032. He is said to have built the city of Karnâvati, which I believe to be the present ruined town of Kâri Talai, which is still called *Karnpur*. Its temples also are said to have been built by

---

43 *Bombay Asiat. Society's Journal*, iv. 97.

Raja Karna Dahariya. He was contemporary with *Kirtti Varma*, the Chandella Raja of Jejâhuti, who reigned from A.D. 1065 to 1100. The Chedis have now nearly disappeared ; but during the height of their power they formed alliances with the chief Rajput families of pure blood. Thus Alhanâ Devi, the daughter of Vijayah Singh of Mewar, married Raja Gaya Karna of Chedi (A.D. 1115 to 1151), and Someswara Chauhan, Raja of Ajmer, went to Tripura, the capital of the Chedi King of Dâhal, where he married Kârpura Devi, the Raja's daughter, and by her became the father of the famous *Prithvi Raja.*

The following list of the Rajas of Dâhal, or W. Chedi, is compiled from the inscriptions and other sources.

KULACHURIS OF DÂHAL, OR W. CHEDI.

Chedi Era.	A.D.	
	249	Establishment of Era.
271	520	Sankaragana of Chedi.
301	550	Buddha, his son, defeated by Mangalisa Châlukya.
431	680	Haihayas defeated by Vinayâditya Châlukya.
481	730	Haihaya Princess, married Vikramâditya Châlukya.
626	875	KOKALLA I., contemporary of Bhoja Deva of Kanauj.
651	900	Mugdhatunga.
676	925	Yuva Raja Deva.
691	940	Lakshmana, made Lakshmana Sâgar at Bilhari.
716	965	Yuva Raja Deva, contemporary of Vâkpati.
731	980	KOKALLA II. Inscription at Khajurâho.
756	1005	GÂNGGEYA-DEVA, contemporary of Mahmud, A.D. 1030.
786	1035	KARNA-DEVA, C.S. 793 = 1042 A.D.
821	1070	Yaṣah Karna Deva.
856	1105	Gaya Karna Deva, C.S. 902 = 1151 A.D.
902	1151	Nara Sinha Deva, C.S. 907, 909, 926, 928.
930	1179	Jaya Sinha Deva [brother].
932	1181	Vijaya Sinha Deva, C.S. 932 = 1181 A.D.

COINS OF THE KULACHURIS OF DÂHAL OR W. CHEDI.

PLATE VIII. No.	Metal.	Grs.	GÂNGGEYA-DEVA.
1	AV	62	Author, common. See Prinsep's *Antiquities*, i. Pl. XXIV. 1, 2, 3. Seated figure of the goddess *Pârvati*, with four arms, holding up a flower in her upraised right hand; legs crossed, and a nimbus round the head. Sanskrit inscription in three lines, *Srimad Gânggeya Deva*.
2	AV	30	Author, unique. Same type and same legend as No. 1.
3	AV	14	Author, unique. Same type and same legend as No. 1.
4	AR	61	Author, 9 specimens. Same type and same legend as No. 1.
5	AR	7	Author, unique. Same type and same legend as No. 1.
—	Æ	61	Author, 6 specimens. Same type and same legend as No. 1.

These are the only coins yet found of the Kulachuris of Dâhal or W. CHEDI. It is very curious that though none of Ganggeya's successors continued the coinage, yet it was imitated by the Chandellas of Jejahuti, by the Tomars of Delhi, and by the Râhtors of Kanauj. This abstinence on the part of his successors is the more remarkable, as the suite of coins described above seems to form a perfect monetary system in all three metals and of different values that must have been very useful and convenient. The type of the goddess Pârvati, as we see on the seal of Karna Deva, was the special symbol or cognisance of the Kalachuris of *Dâhal.* On the seal the goddess with four arms is represented with an Elephant on each side anointing her, and accompanied by a Bull. Sometimes the Bull was represented alone on the standard as the *Suvarna - vrishabha - dhwaja,* "the golden - bull - standard." But there is no trace of the Bull on the coins.

Kulachuris of Mahâkosala, or E. Chedi.

The Haihaya Kingdom of *Mahâkosala*, or *E. Chedi*, comprised all the country of the head-waters of the Mahanadi River and its tributaries. It is noticed by the Chinese pilgrim, Hwen Thsang, in the seventh century, when its King was a Kshatriya named *Satavâhana*. But there is no name like this in the lists of the *Haihaya-vamsi* Rajahs of Ratanpur and Raypur. The Chronicles can only be accepted when they agree with the information which is found in the inscriptions. Ratanpur is the earliest capital mentioned in the inscriptions. But the chief cities of the country of the Mahanadi, which I have myself visited, are certainly *Râjim*, *Sirpur*, and *Seorinârâyan*, all on the Mahanadi. At these three places there are many magnificent temples and ancient inscriptions to attest the former power and wealth of the rulers of the country.

Something like real history appears to begin with *Sura Deva* of the Chronicles, who is said to have conquered Telingâna. His date is given as *about* A.D. 749, but as all the dates of his successors are recorded in the *Chedi era*, his true date will be about 749 + 249 = 998 A.D. or 1000. The earliest inscription that I have seen is dated in C.S. 866, or A.D. 1115. In it I find mention of Sri Kârtavîrya, Haihaya, Sri Kokalla Chedîṣwara, Ratna Râja, Prithvi Deva, Jâjalla Deva. (See Kielhorn, *Epigraphia Indica*, i. p. 33.)

A second inscription dated in Samvat 1207, or A.D. 1150, gives the names of Jâjalla Deva Chedinarendra, Ratna Deva, Prithvi Deva.

Two other inscriptions give Prithvi Deva Chedikula, and the later dates of A.D. 1159 and 1168.

Comparing these names with those recorded in the native Chronicles I make out the following list of the—

RAJAS OF MAHAKOSALA OR E. CHEDI.

A.D.	Inscriptions.	Chronicles.
		Sura Deva
1000	Kokalla [? Kokalla II.]	Prithvi Deva
1030	Ratna Deva	Brahma Deva
1060	Prithvi Deva	Rudra Deva
1090	Jâjalla Deva, A.D. 1115	Jâjalla Deva
1120	Ratna Deva	Ratna Deva
1140	Prithvi Deva, A.D. 1145-1168	Vira Sinha Deva
		Ratna Sinha Deva

Up to the present year the only known coins of Mahâkosala or E. Chedi were those of Prithvi Deva, and they were, as I believe, known to myself alone. It is true that E. Thomas has twice referred to some gold coins of Prithvi Deva, but both times he has ingeniously avoided to describe the obverse.

In his first accounts (*Prinsep's Essays*, i. 395) he says that when he mentioned the coins of Prithvi Deva, in vol. i., p. 292, he had overlooked the fact that Prinsep had read the name of Prithvi Deva. But the name which Prinsep read was on a "unique *copper* coin of Cunningham's," and not on a *gold* coin which Thomas describes as "sufficiently common, hitherto unpublished."

Again, in his Pathân kings, p. 19, he refers to the *gold* coin in the following terms :

> *Gold*—Prinsep's Essays, i. 292, common.
> Obverse.—*As usual* (!) "*Srimat Prithvi Deva.*"

In both instances he carefully avoids any description of the obverse, except by the strange and mysterious words "*as usual.*" But what did he mean by *as usual?* Did he mean the seated goddess?

The fact is he was writing from memory of what I had

told him, and had not actually seen the coins which I had seen in the British Museum—six specimens in gold of *Srimat Prithvi Deva.* I had never seen even one gold specimen before, and I now believe that Thomas was inaccurate in his description of them as common. To my knowledge these six coins in the British Museum were the only known *gold* specimens of Prithvi Deva until the present year, when Dr. Hoërnle has described a seventh.

I have entered into this explanation because Dr. Hoërnle has been misled by Thomas, whose account he quotes[44] as "Prithvi Deva *gold* coins are sufficiently common." On the contrary, the *gold* coins of Prithvi Deva are very rare, and his copper coins still rarer, the only specimens of the latter known to me being two coins in my own collection. On these two copper coins the figure of the obverse is Hanumân with four arms, which is accurately described by James Prinsep (E. Thomas, i., p. 395) as "the four-handed god crushing a demon." But this is certainly not the type of the *six gold* coins in the British Museum, of which the casts are now lying before me. From Dr. Hoërnle's description of the obverse of the *seventh gold* coin (found this year in the Central Provinces) I gather that he takes the obverse figure to be Hanumân. His words are "the figure (of Hanumân) is *fairly distinct* on the *gold* coin." I conjecture that he has adopted this opinion from Prinsep's etching of my *copper* coin, for I cannot make out any trace of Hanumân on any of the six coins in the British Museum. In fact, I have not been able to make out any definite figure amongst the confusion of shapeless objects on these coins.[45] I consider

[44] *Proceedings Bengal Asiatic Society*, April and May, 1893, p. 93.

[45] [This confused type may perhaps be intended to represent a lion, facing r., rampant. The coins of Jâjalla Deva and Ratna

that Thomas's description of "as usual" refers to the "seated goddess."

COINS OF THE KULACHURIS OF MAHAKOSALA OR E. CHEDI.

PLATE VIII.

No.	Metal.	Grs.	
			PRITHVI-DEVA. A.D. 1060—1090.
6	AV	59·5	British Museum. 6 specimens from Payne Knight's collection. A number of confused shapeless objects, surrounded by a circle of dots. Indian inscription in two lines of large letters, *Srimat Prithvi Deva.*
7	Æ	84	Author, unique; obtained in 1885. Four-armed male figure, holding different indistinct objects in his hands. Indian inscription, same as on the gold coin.
8	Æ	107	Author, unique; obtained in 1885. Four-armed figure of Hanumân with right foot trampling on a prostrate figure. Indian inscription, same as on the gold coin.
			JÂJALLA DEVA, A.D. 1090—1120.
9	Æ	57·5	Indian Museum, Calcutta; found in 1893. Large coins, 9. (*Brit. Mus.*) Very crude figure of Hanumân [Dr. Höernle]. Indian inscription, *Srimaj Jâjalla Deva.*
10	Æ	14	Indian Museum, 17 specimens, small; same type as last. (*Brit. Mus.*)
			RATNA-DEVA, A.D. 1120—1140.
11	Æ	14	Indian Museum, 29 specimens, all small. (*Brit. Mus.*) Very crude figure of Hanumân [Dr. Höernle]. Indian inscription, *Srimat Ratna Deva.*

CHANDELLAS OF JEJÂHUTI OR MAHOBA.

Jejâhuti, or *Jejâkabhukti*, the territory of the Chandellas, is also known by the name of its capital city of *Mahoba* or

---

Deva figured in the plate have recently been presented to the British Museum by the Government of India, through the Asiatic Society of Bengal.—E. J. R.]

Mahotsava. It comprised all the country lying between the Jumna on the north and the sources of the Kiyân or Ken River on the south, and from the Dhasân River on the west to the Vindhya Mountains on the east. The Ken River (or Karnavati) runs through the country from south to north, dividing it into two nearly equal portions, with the capital cities of Mahoba and Khajurâho in the western half, and the great forts of Kâlanjar and Ajaygarh in the eastern half. Its area was upwards of 12,000 square miles. Its wealth may be judged by the magnificent group of Temples still existing at Khajurâho, and its power may be judged by its conquest of Kanauj, and its defiance of Mahmud of Ghazni.

The popular traditions of the people as detailed in the Mahoba-Khand derive their origin from Chandrama, or the Moon, by Hemâvatî, the daughter of Hemraj, the family priest of the Raja of Benares. But this popular tradition receives no support from the inscriptions, which assign them to the Chandrâtreya line. In the two long inscriptions of Khajurâho the earliest name mentioned is that of Nannuka, six generations before *Dhanga Deva*, whose date we know to be A.D. 953 to 999, and in Dhanga's own copper-plate the earliest name recorded is that of his own grandfather, Harsha Deva.

The chief facts in the history of the Chandels have been given in my Archæological Survey Reports, but more particularly in my latest account in vol. xxi, in which I have recorded all the known inscriptions of the family, with a detailed list of the kings, and a summary of their history. The earliest coins are those of *Kîrtti Varma,* the antagonist of the Kalachuri *Karna Deva* of Chedi, to whom he was at one time tributary. His coins are of gold only, but of several of the later Princes there are both gold and copper coins. Only one silver coin has yet been found of

Jaya Varma. The larger gold coins generally weigh upwards of sixty grains, rising to sixty-three; the smaller gold coins are of fifteen grains. The type is the same of all the gold coins. On the obverse the goddess Parvati seated, copied from the money of Gânggeya Devá of Chedi. The copper coins are of the same weights as the gold, sixty and fifteen grains, but their obverse type is a figure of Hanumân.

The larger gold coins are therefore golden *drammas*, and the smaller ones ¼-*drammas*.

CHANDELLAS OF JEJÂHUTI OR MAHOBA.

No.	Date.		Names.	Inscriptions.
	V.Sam.	A.D.		
1	857	800	Nannuka Deva	
2	882	825	Vâkpati	
3		850	Vijaya	
4		875	Râhila	
5		900	Harsha Deva	
6		925	Yaşo Varma Deva	
7	1010	958	DHANGA-DEVA	s. 1011—1055
8	1056	999	GANDA-DEVA	s. 1056
9	1082	1025	Vidyâdhara Deva	
10	1097	1040	Vijaya Pâla Deva	
11	1107	1050	Deva Varma Deva	s. 1107
12	1120	1063	Kîrtti Varma Deva	s. 1154
13	1155	1097	Hallakshana Varma Deva	
14	1167	1110	Jaya Varma Deva	s. 1173
15	1177	1120	Hallakshana Varma Deva	
16	1179	1122	Prithvi Varma Deva	
17	1186	1129	Madana Varma Deva	s. 1186—1220
18	1222	1165	Paramârdi Deva	s. 1224
19	1268	1203	Trailokya Varma Deva	s. 1269—1297
20	1297	1240	Vîra Varma I.	s. 1312—1337
21	1339	1282	Bhoja Varma	s. 1345
22	1357	1350	Vîra Varma II.	s. 1372
30	1577	1520	Kirat Singh [Kirtti]	

COINS OF THE CHANDELLAS OF JEJÂHUTI OR MAHOBA.

PLATE VIII. No.	Metal.	Grs.	
			KIRTTI-VARMMA, A.D. 1063—1097.
12	AV	63	Author, rare. *Goddess Pârvatî* with four arms seated. Indian legend in two lines, *Srimat Kirtti Varmma Deva.*
13	AV	31	Author, same type and legend as No. 12.
			HALLAKSHANA VARMMA-DEVA, 1097—1110, A.D.
14	AV	63	Author, rare. *Goddess Pârvatî*, with four arms, seated. Indian legend, *Srimat Hallakshana Varmma Deva.*
15	AV	15	Author, same type and legend as No. 14.
16	Æ	61	Author, rare. Hanumân under a canopy. Indian legend as on No. 14.
			JAYA-VARMMA-DEVA, A.D. 1110—1120.
17	Æ	60	Author, six specimens. Hanumân as on No. 16. Indian legend, *Srimaj Jaya Varmma Deva.*
			PRITHVI-VARMMA-DEVA, A.D. 1122—1129.
18	Æ	41	Author. Hanumân, as No. 16. Indian legend, *Srimat Prithvi Varmma Deva.*
			MADANA-VARMMA-DEVA, A.D. 1129—1165.
19	AV	61	Author. Goddess Pârvati, with four arms, seated. Indian legend, *Sriman-Madana Varmma Deva.*
20	AV	15	Author, same type and legend as No. 19.
21	Æ	15	Author, a worn coin. Hanumân, as before. Indian legend as on No. 19.
			PARAMARDDI-DEVA, A.D. 1165—1203.
—	AV		*See* Dr. Höernle, *Journal Asiatic Society, Bengal*, 1889, Plate IV.

PLATE VIII. No.	Metal.	Grs.	
			Goddess Pârvati, with four arms, seated. Indian legend, *Sri-m* [not distinct]. N.B.—I possess four *copper* coins which appear to bear the same legend, but I cannot read it satisfactorily, *Sri-mad Va sava Matya na Deva* or *Sri mat Ke sava Mahi — Deva.*
			VIRA-VARMMA-I, A.D. 1240—1282.
—	AV		*See* Dr. Höernle, in the same Journal. Goddess Pârvati, with four arms, as before. Indian legend, *Srimad Vîra Varmma Deva.*

IX.—TOMARS OF DELHI AND KANAUJ.

According to the universally accepted tradition the city of *Indraprastha*, which had lain waste for seven hundred and ninety-two years, from the time of Vikramâditya, was refounded by Anang Pâl, a Tomara Rajput, and named *Dilhi* (the *Delhi* of the present day), according to a legend which refers to the *Iron Pillar*.[46] The date is differently stated by some writers; but they only differ by a few years from Vikr. Samvat 792, or A.D. 735. But the kingdom of Delhi is not referred to by any of the early Muhammadan writers, and the first mention of it is during the campaigns of Muhammad Ibn Sâm in the end of the twelfth century. Masudi, who travelled in the East in A.H. 332 = A.D. 943, does not notice Delhi; but he knows Kanauj, whose kings had the common title of *Bovara* or *Povara*, which I take to represent *Tovara* or *Tomara*, which was the family name of the kings of Delhi.

When Kanauj was captured by Mahmud of Ghazni in A.D. 1022, the reigning king, according to Utbi, was named *Râj Pâl*, or *Râjaipâl*, which I take to be Raja *Jaipâl*, who

[46] See *Archæol. Survey*, i. 171, where the legend is given at full length.

PLATE IX.

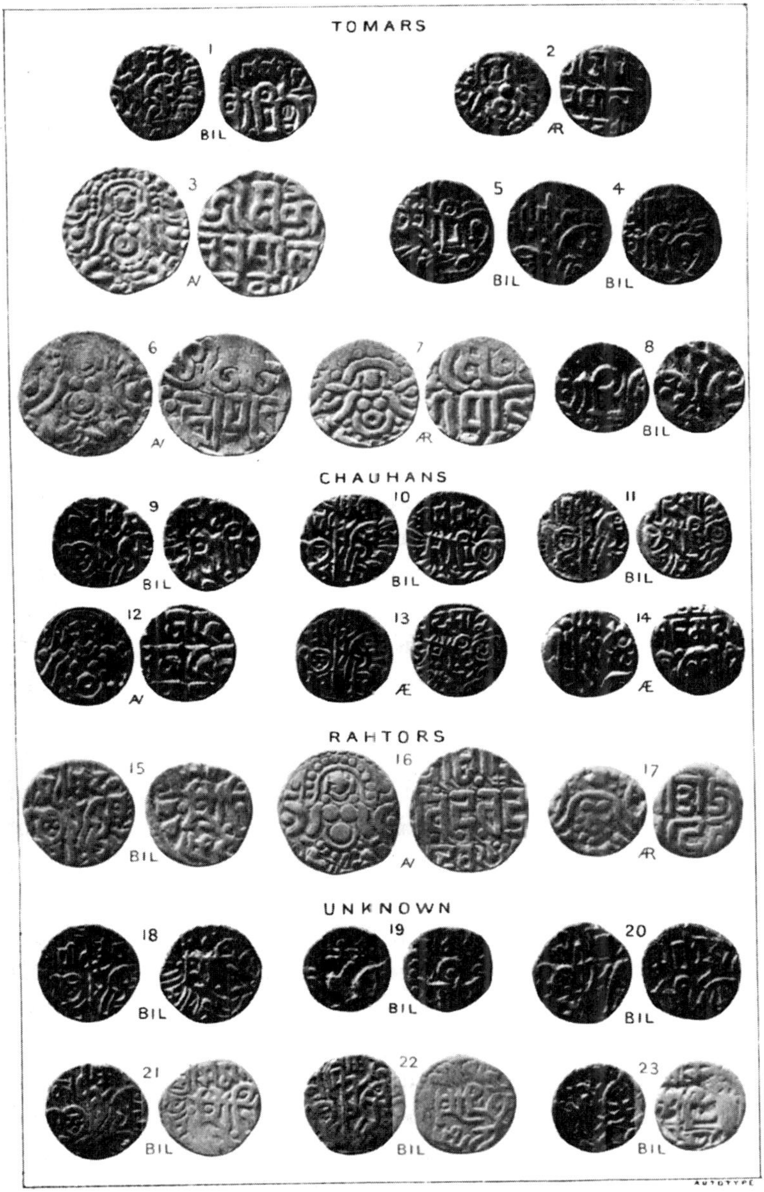

DELHI AND KANAUJ.

at this very time was the *Tomar* Raja of Delhi. On account of his submission to Mahmud he was attacked and killed by Ganda, the Chandel Raja of Kâlanjâr. He was succeeded by *Kumâr Pâl*, whose name is also found in the list of the Tomar Rajas of Delhi, immediately following that Raja *Jaipál*. Next to him is *Anangpâl*, who is recorded to have built the fort of *Lâlkot* at Delhi, which is thus recorded by the annalist in Samvat 1117 or A.D. 1060—

Dilli ki kot karâya
Lâl kot kahâya.

As Kanauj was conquered by the Rahtor Chandra Deva about A.D. 1050, I conjecture that, after the death of Kumâra Pâla, his successor the Tomar Raja Anang-Pâl must have retired to Delhi, where he built the fort mentioned by the annalist.

The *Tomars*, or *Toärs*, are one of the high-class Rajput class, who have intermarried with the Sisodias of Mewar. The Tomars of Gwalior held that fortress from A.D. 1375 till 1518, when Vikramâditya, the last Raja, was conquered by Ibrahim Lodi. The northern district of the Gwalior territory still bears the name of *Toär-gâr*, and a large district to the south of Delhi is named *Toär-vati*.

In drawing up a list of the Rajas of the several different families which have successively ruled over Delhi and Kanauj, I think it will be convenient to have them so arranged that their successions may be seen at a glance.

The *Tomar* family is admitted by all the authorities to have been established by Anangpâl I., who founded Delhi in Vikr. Sam. 792 or A.D. 736. The same date is given in another era on the Iron Pillar at Delhi, as *Sam.* 418 *Raj Tuṅwar Âdi Aṅang*. Taking this date as recorded in the Gupta era, it will be 418 + 318 = 736 A.D. The oldest written authority that I can find is Amir Khusru the Poet, who lived under Muhammed Khilji in A.D. 1300. Speaking of Anangpâl I., he calls him "a great Rai who lived five hundred or six hundred years ago, that is between A.D. 700 and 800."[47]

I have already quoted the statement of Masudi (A.D. 930—948) that the reigning family of Kanauj were Povaras (read Tovaras). I may also quote the statement of Alberuni, that Kanauj was rendered famous by the *Pândavas*, as Mathurâ was by Vâsu Deva.[48] Now as the *Tomaras* were *Pândavas*, while their immediate predecessors in Kanauj were *Raghuvansis*, and their immediate successors were Rahtors, the statements of Alberuni can only apply to the Tomaras who reigned between them. But when we find that the names of these Tomaras are absolutely identical with those of the rulers of Kanauj at that very time, and moreover are recorded in the same order, there can be little doubt of their identity. These names are—

Jaypâl, reigning when Mahmud took Kanauj.
Kunwarpâl, placed on the throne as his successor.
Anangpâl II., founder of Lâlkot, after loss of Kanauj.

With these identifications the chain of evidence seems to be complete.

Of the Raghuvansis, Bhoja Deva, and his successors who call themselves kings of Mahodaya or Kanauj, I have already spoken. The last of these Princes of whom we have any record is Devapâla, whose latest date is A.D. 948. The earliest Tomara Raja of whom we have coins is *Salakshuna-pâla*, whose date is A.D. 978.

The successors of the Tomars were the Rahtors, who, under their leader Chandra Deva, conquered Kanauj about A.D. 1050, or perhaps a few years later, as Anangpâl II.

---

[47] H. M. Elliot, iii. 565.

[48] Sachau's *Alberuni*, i. 199; Rashid ud din says the same, H. M. Elliot, i. 54.

is said to have founded Lâlkot at Delhi in A.D. 1060. There are no coins or inscriptions of the conqueror Chandra Deva, but we have an inscription of his son Madana Pâla, dated in s. 1154 or A.D. 1097, and an inscription of his grandson Govinda Chandra Deva, dated in s. 1177 or A.D. 1120, when he was a young man; and from these I calculate that Madana Pâl's accession may be assigned to A.D. 1080, and Chandra Deva's accession about A.D. 1050, allowing twenty-five years to each generation. This would place the conquest of Kanauj by the Rahtors soon after A.D. 1050.

Of the *Chauhâns* we have got the only trustworthy account from their inscriptions. The Prithvi Râj Râsau is a forgery, as shown by Dr. Bühler,[49] and Tod's list and the Bardic chronicles, which were derived from Chand, are consequently worthless. Dr. Bühler quotes the two inscriptions of V.S. 1030 and V.S. 1225, and the *Prithivirâja-Vijaya*, written by a Kashmiri Pundit, as giving the true genealogy. To these I may add my own Madanpur inscription, which gives both the genealogy and the date of the conquest of *Jejâkabhukti*, or Jejâhuti, in a few lines.[50]

> *Aum! Aruno-rājasya pautrena Sri,*
> *Someswarasununā Jejāka-*
> *bhuktidesoyam Prithvirājena*
> *lunitaḥ S.* 1239.

From this we learn that the conquest of Jejâhuti (or Mahoba) took place in s. 1239 or A.D. 1182.

According to the *Prithivirâja Vijaya*, Aruno had three sons:

1. *Nameless*, who murdered his father	2. Visala Deva, or Vigraha Raja	3. Someswara
|	|	|
Prithivi Bhaṭa	No son	Prithivi Raja

[49] *Asiat. Society of Bengal Proceedings*, 1893, pp. 93, 94.
[50] *Archæol. Survey of India*, xxi. 174.

We have coins of *Someswara* and of *Prithivi Raja;* but I know of none of *Visala* (or *Vigraha*) or of the nephew *Prithivi Bhaṭa.* And no coins have yet been found of *Aruno* (or *Avella Deva*). The kingdom of *Visala Deva* is called *Sâkambhari* (Sambhar) in the Delhi Pillar inscription; and in the Prithivirâja-Vijaya the kingdom of the Chauhâns is said to be Ajayamera or Ajmer. In the Hammîra Mahâkâvya it is called *Sapâdalaksha* (Sawâlak) of which *Ajmer* and *Hânsi* were the acknowledged capitals. I have visited all these places, but I have never found any coins which I could assign to *Aruno* or to *Visala.* I have, however, several coins with strange names which I believe to belong to the Chauhâns of Ajmer.

Rajas of Delhi and Kanauj.

A.D.	TOMARS.	RAGHU-VANSIS.		RAHTORS.	
736	ANANG-PÂL I.				
753					
772					
793					
813					
833		835	Ramabhadra Deva		
848					
874			BHOJA-DEVA		
895					
918					
939	Sukhpal (or Tejpal)				
960	Gopâl				
978	Sallakshanpâl				
1003	Jaipâl				
1019	Kumâr Pâl				
1049	ANANGA-PÂL II.			1050	CHANDRA-DEVA
1079	Vijaya Pal (or Tej Pâl)			1080	Madan Pâl
1103	Mahi Pâl			1115	Govinda Chandra
1128	ANANGA-PÂL III.				
1149				1165	Jaya Chandra
	CHAUHANS.				
1120?	Aruno Raja				
1150?	VISALA, 1162 } brothers				
1162	Someswara } brothers				
1166	Prithvi Raja				
1191				1193	

COINS OF THE TOMARS OF DELHI AND KANAUJ.

PLATE IX. No.	Metal.	Grs.	
			SALLAKSHANA-PALA DEVA, A.D. 978—1003.
1	Bil.		Author; E. Thomas, *Pathân Kings*, p. 62. Wrongly attributed to Kabul. Horseman carrying lance to right; copied from coins of Brahman Kings of Kabul. Indian legend, *Sri Sallakshana Pâla Deva.* Recumbent humped Bull. *Sri Sâmanta Deva.*
			AJAYA-PALA-DEVA, A.D. 1003—1019.
2	Æ		Author. Four-armed figure of Lakshmi seated. Copied from Chedi coins of Gânggeya Deva. *Rev.*—Indian legend in three lines, *Sri Ajaya Pâla Deva.*
			KUMÂRA-PÂLA-DEVA, A.D. 1019—1049.
3	AV		Author; several of these coins came from Kabul. Four-armed figure of Lakshmi seated. *Rev.*—Indian legend in three lines, *Srimat Kumâra Pâla Deva.*
			ANANGA-PÂLA-DEVA, A.D. 1049—1079.
4	Bil.		Author. Horseman with lance. *Sri Ananga Pâla Deva.*
5	Bil.		Recumbent humped Bull. *Mâdhava Sri Sâmanta Deva.*
			MAHI-PÂLA, A.D. 1103—1128.
6	AV		Author. Four-armed figure of Lakshmi seated. Indian legend, *Srimat Mahipâla Deva.*
7	Æ		Author. Type and legend same as on No. 6.
8	Bil.		Author. Recumbent humped Bull. *Sri Mahipâla Deva.* Horseman.

COINS OF THE CHAUHANS OF AJMER AND DELHI.

PLATE IX. No.	Metal.	Grs.	
			SOMESWARA DEVA, A.D. 1162—1166.
9	Bil.	53	Author; E. Thomas, *Pathâns*, p. 63; *Ariana Antiqua*, xix. 28. Horseman with lance to right. *Sri Someswara Deva.* Recumbent humped Bull. *Asâwari Sri Sâmanta Deva.*
			PRITHVI RAJA DEVA, A.D. 1166—1192.
10	Bil.	52	Author; E. Thomas, *Pathâns*, p. 64; *Ariana Antiqua*, xix. 18. Horseman with lance to right. *Sri Prithvi Raja Deva.* Recumbent Bull, humped. *Asâwari Sri Sâmanta Deva.*
			PRITHVI RAJA and MUHAMMAD bin SAM, A.D. 1192.[51]
11	Bil.		Author, three specimens; E. Thomas, *Pathâns*, p. 11. Horseman with lance to right. *Sri Prithvi Raja.* Recumbent humped Bull. *Sri Mahamad Sâme.*
			MUHAMMAD bin SÂM.
12	*AV*		Author; *Ariana Antiqua*, xxi. 25; E. Thomas, *Pathâns*, p. 20. Lakshmi with four arms seated. Copied from the coins of Govinda Chandra. Indian legend in three lines, *Sri Mahamad bênê Sâm.*

[51] The occurrence of these two names on the same coin is to be explained by the facts related by *Minhaj*, who assigns the *capitulation* of Delhi to the year A.H. 587 (A.D. 1191), when Prithvi Raja became *tributary*. Aibek then retired to Hânsi, but returned to Delhi in A.H. 589 (A.D. 1193) and captured the city. I assign these coins to the intermediate year A.H. 588 = A.D. 1192.

PLATE IX.

No.	Metal.	Grs.	
13	Æ		Author; E. Thomas, *Pathâns*, Pl. I., 9; p. 15. Horseman with lance. *Sri Hamirah.* Copied from coins of Prithvi Raja. Recumbent humped Bull. *Sri Mahamad Sâme.*
14	Æ		Author; E. Thomas, *Pathâns*, Pl. I., 10; p. 16. Rude execution. Horseman with lance. *Sri Hamirah.* Recumbent humped Bull. *Sri Mahamad Sâme.*

COINS OF THE RAHTORS OF KANAUJ.

No.	Metal.	Grs.	
			MADANA PÂLA DEVA, A.D. 1080—1115.
15	Bil.		Author; E. Thomas, *Pathâns*, p. 62; *Ariana Antiqua*, xix. 19. Horseman with lance to right. *Sri Madana Pâla Deva.* Recumbent humped Bull. *Mâdhava Sri Sâmanta Deva.*
			GOVINDA CHANDRA DEVA, A.D. 1115—1165.
16	AV		Author; E. Thomas, *Pathâns*, p. 19. Lakshmi with four arms seated. Copied from coins of Gânggeya Deva of Chedi. Indian legend, *Srimad Govinda Chandra Deva.*
			AJAYA-CHANDRA (Jay-chand), A.D. 1165—1193.
17	AR		Author, nine specimens. Lakshmi with four arms seated. Indian legend, *Sri Ajaya Deva.*

UNKNOWN RAJPUT COINS.

Very little can be said of any one of these coins, as the names are all more or less imperfect, and their complete readings can therefore only be guessed. E. Thomas has

PLATE IX. No.	Metal.	Grs.	
			given four of them tentatively, and with his readings I partly agree. My readings are taken from my own coins.
			Pîpala.
18	Bil.		Author, three specimens, E. Thomas, *Pathâns*, p. 59. *Horseman. Sri Pîpala.* *Humped Bull. Kutâmâna Sri Samanta Deva.* All my specimens agree in this reading on the Bull side, but E. Thomas reads only *Asâwari Sri Samanta Deva.* Chand mentions *Pîpa Parihâr* Raja of Sâmbhar. I found the same name in the books of *Mûk-ji*, the Bard of the Khichi Chauhâns. There was also a *Pipanjar* Raja in the same books.
19	Bil.		Author, unique. Horseman. *Sri Jâ+ +* Recumbent Bull. *Sri Samanta.*
20	Bil.		Author, unique. Horseman. + *Bhikh* + + (or *Bhishma*). Recumbent Bull. *Sri Sâmanta Deva.*
21	Bil.		Author, one coin; E. Thomas, *Pathâns*, p. 59, three coins. Horseman. *Kîl* + E. T. has *Sri Kîlli Deva.* Recumbent Bull. + *pâla Sri Sâmanta Deva.* E. T. reads the same, p. 59.
22	Bil.		Author, unique. Horseman. *Sri Hamirah.* Recumbent Bull. *Mau* + *Sri Uvâme ?*
23	Bil.		Author, two coins; E .Thomas, *Pathâns*, p. 59. Horseman. *Sri* + + Recumbent Bull. *Sri Kalhana* or *Kilhana ?* On the saddle-cloth Persian legend.
—	Bil.		Author, two coins, not in Plate; E. Thomas, *Pathâns*, p. 59. Horseman. *Sri Pîthî* + + Recumbent Bull. *Raja Sri Samanta.* My second coin, *Asâwari Sri Samanta;* as E. T. has it.

PLATE X

NARWAR AND MEWAR.

The Billon coins of mixed silver and copper, which were adopted by all the later kings of the Tomaras and Chauhans, are called *Diliwâls* or *Diliâls* by the early Muhammadan writers. They were copied by Muhammad bin Sâm and his successor; but the native Hindu name is not known. Neither is their exact value known; but I believe that after the *silver tangkas* came into use in the reign of *Iltitmish*, the *Diliâls* became the *jitals* or *chitals* of 40 and 50 to the tangka. Taking the silver in each as 2·8 grains, the fifty pieces would contain 120 grains of silver, and 50 times 50, or 2,500 grains of copper. Allowing 50 rates of copper, the quantity of this metal would be worth 50 of silver and the 50 diliâls would therefore be worth 170 grains of silver, or just one silver tangka.

X.—Rajputs of Narwar.

The coins assigned to the mediæval Rajas of Narwar are found chiefly at Narwar itself and in the neighbouring cities of Jhânsi and Gwalior. The assignment is confirmed by the discovery of inscriptions giving the genealogy of five princes of the family, from *Châhaṛa Deva* down to Ganapati. But we have coins of an earlier king, *Malaya Varmma Deva*, who, though not mentioned either in history or in the inscriptions, must have ruled at Narwar, as his coins are found along with those of the recorded kings. They also bear dates in Samvat years, as we find on the coins of the known Rajas of Narwar, Châhaṛa Deva, Asalla Deva, and Ganapati Deva.

The following list of the Rajas of Narwar has been drawn up from the inscriptions and from the dates furnished by the coins and other sources:—

RAJAHS OF NALAPURA OR NARWAR.

Accession.			Dates from Inscriptions and Coins.
Sam.	A.D.		
		Malaya Varmma Deva	s. 1280, 82, 83, 90
1294	1237	Châhaḍa Deva	s. 129-, 1303, 1305, 1306, 1311
1312	1255	Nṛi Varmma	
1312	1255	Asalla Deva	s. 1327, 1330
1335	1278	Gopâla	s. 1337
1347	1290	Gaṇapati	s. 1348, 1355

The inscriptions relating to the Rajas of Narwar were found at the following places :—

No. 1 at *Raï*, dated S. 1327 = A.D. 1270, in time of Âsalla Deva.

No. 2 at *Dahi*, dated S. 1337 = A.D. 1280, mentioning Gopâla Raja.

No. 3 at *Sarwaya*, dated S. 1248 = A.D. 1291, in time of Gaṇapati Raja.

No. 4 at *Narwar*, dated S. 1255 = A.D. 1298, in time of Gaṇapati.

Of *Malaya Varmma Deva* we know nothing except his date which we gather from his coins. From his name of Varmma I was at first inclined to look upon him as of a different family ; but as Châhaḍa Deva's son was named Nri-Varmma, this Malaya may have belonged to the Narwar family.

Of Châhaṛa Deva we have two apparently conflicting accounts both related by the same writer, Minhâj, in his Tabakât-i-Nâsiri. As he was a contemporary, I am inclined to adopt his accounts, and to make an attempt to reconcile them.

According to the earlier accounts *Râna Châhar Achârí,*

of Ranthanbhor and the Koh-payah of Mewât, was defeated by the Muhammadan general, Tâbasi, sent from Delhi in A.H. 631 or 632 = A.D. 1234 or 1235, at the end of the reign of Iltitmish. He is described as the "*most noble and illustrious of all the Rais of Hindustan.*"[52] He is also called Nâhar Deo.

In the later accounts of A.H. 649 = A.D, 1251, *Châhar Deo Achâri* was defeated by Ulughkhan on his return from the plunder of Kâlanjar, at the defiles of the Sindh River near the fortress of Narwar. He is in this account called "*the greatest of the Rais of all that part of the country.*"[53]

Major Raverty, the translator of the Tabakât, thinks that two different Hindu chiefs are intended, while E. Thomas confidently identifies them as one and the same person.[54] Major Raverty's opinion is not without support, but I feel inclined to agree with Thomas. I found my conclusion on the title of *Achâri*, which is given to the Rantanbhor Chahâr Deo in this account, and to the Narwar Chahâr Deo in all the accounts. Much speculation has been spent in trying to explain this title. It sometimes is written *Chahâr-i-Achâri*, or "*Chahâr of Achâri*," but no place of this name is known. As *Chahâr-Achâri*, it has been supposed to designate the Raja as an *Achârya*, or "religious teacher." In my opinion it is only an attempt to represent in Persian characters the title of *Asâwari*, which is found on the Raja's own coins as the independent ruler of Rantanbhor, "*Asâwari Sri Samanta Deva*," and then as the tributary under *Shams-*

---

[52] Raverty's Translation, pp. 791 and 824.
[53] Raverty, p. 824.
[54] *Pathâns*, pp. 67—70.

ud-din Iltitmish as "*Asâwari Sri Samasorala Deva.*" [55] Now this title of *Achâri*, although it does not appear on the Narwar coins, is always given to the Raja Chahâr Deo of that place.

I conclude that Chahâr Deo latterly took up his residence at Narwar, which, according to the inscriptions, was his birthplace. His Narwar coins begin with one date in 129*x* Samvat, the unit figure being gone. If taken as S. 1291 the date would be A.D. 1234 in the last year of Iltitmish. But as I have one coin of Malaya Varmma Deva dated 129*x*, Chahâr Deo's date may be taken as late as S. 1294 = A.D. 1237.

COINS OF THE RAJPUTS OF NARWAR.

PLATE X. No.	Metal.	Grs.	
			MALAYA-VARMMA-DEVA, A.D. 1280.
1	Æ		Author, 18 specimens. Rude copy of horseman. Indian legend, *Sri Malaya Varmma Deva*, S. 1280.
2	Æ		Author, type same as No. 1. *Sri Malaya Varmma Deva*, S. 83.
3	Æ		Author, type same as No. 1, date, S. 9+, unit figure lost.
			CHAHAḌA-DEVA, A.D. 1234—1255.
4	Æ		Author, 12 specimens, mixed silver and copper; E. Thomas, *Pathâns*, p. 70. Horseman to right. *Sri Châhaḍa Deva.* Recumbent humped Bull. *Asâwari Sri Samasorala Deva.*
—	Æ		*Ariana Antiqua*, Pl. xix., 16; E. Thomas, *Pathâns*, p. 70. Same as No. 4, but reverse legend, *Asâwari Sri Samanta Deva.*

[55] E. Thomas, *Pathâns*, p. 70.

PLATE X.

No.	Metal.	Grs.	
5	Æ		Author, copper coins, 14 specimens. Rude horseman, no legend. Legend in three lines, *Srimat Châhada Deva*, S. 129+, unit lost.
6	Æ		Author, same types as No. 5, S. 1303.
7	Æ		Author, same types, S. 1311.
			ASALLA-DEVA, A.D. 1255—1278.
8	Æ		Author, 8 specimens. Rude horseman to right, scarcely traceable. Legend in three lines, *Srimat Asala Deva*, S. 1330.
9	Æ		Author, same types, S. 1312.
			GAṆAPATI DEVA, A.D. 1347.
10	Æ		Author, unique. Rude horseman, scarcely traceable. Legend in three lines, *Srimat Gaṇapati Deva*, S. 134+, unit figure lost.

RAJPUTS OF MEḌAPÂTA OR MEWÂR.

Medapâṭa or *Mewâr*, the most southerly of the great Rajput kingdoms, comprises all the country on the upper course of the *Varṇanâsa* or Banâs River, including a compact territory upwards of 200 miles in length from north to south, by more than 100 miles in breadth from east to west. Its ancient capital was *Chitrâwar* or *Chitor*, which is still the great stronghold of the kingdom; but its present capital is *Udaypur*, which is now the common name for the principality.

Its rulers have long been known as one of the highest caste Rajputs, the *Gobhilas* or *Guhilas*, whose traditional history begins with *Bappa Râwal*. According to the records of the family *Bappa Râwal* captured Chitor from a *Mori* chief in the year S. 191. This is the date recorded in the books of Mukji, the Khichi bard, which I examined myself, and which Mukji's sons corroborated by repeating a verse beginning with *Eka sao angkânbî*, (*Ek sau ekânawî*,) "In the year one hundred and ninety-one," and ending with "Bappa Râwal his kingdom won." This date I should refer to the Harsha era of A.D. 607, which would give 606 + 191 = 797 A.D. Tod gives A.D. 727, but does not say how he obtained it.

We have no coins that can be assigned to any of the early Rânas of Mewâr. It is probable that coins were struck by some of them; but as they would be of Sassanian type, without names or with only single letters, none can be assigned.

It is possible that some of the unassigned Horseman and Bull coins of Plate IX. might belong to the Rânas who were contemporary with Prithvi Raja Chauhân. We might expect to find specimens of *Samara Sinha*, the Gobhila son-in-law of Prithvi Raja, but none have appeared. Perhaps the last coin in Plate IX., fig. 23, may belong to Samara Sinha's son, *Karana* or *Kalhana*.

But the first coins that can be assigned with certainty to Mewâr are the two square pieces in Plate X. figs. 11, 12, which bear the name of Râna *Kumbhakarṇa*, or *Kumbho*, the founder of the hill-fortress of *Kumbhalmer*. These pieces are of historical interest, as they must be specimens of the actual *tangkas*, coined in his own name by Râna Kumbho, which gave so much offence when offered to the Muhammadan invader, Mahmud I. of Malwa. Ferishta, who relates the story, says that when Mahmud reached Chitor,[56] Râna Kumbho, in order to avert the approaching calamity, met the king on the road, and made a large offering of money (*tankas*) *coined in his own*

---

[56] Briggs's *Ferishta*, iv. 221.

name, which so incensed Mahmud that he returned the whole sum. But some time afterwards Mahmud accepted 10 lakhs of *tankas*, without any scruple, from the same king.[57] The fact is, that when the Muhammadan prince was successful, he was insolent and overbearing; but when he was obliged to raise the siege of Chitor, he became milder in his conduct, and was glad to receive the money as a present. The Hindus, however, looked upon the raising of the siege as a confession of defeat, and Râna Kumbho erected in commemoration his graceful Pillar of Victory in the fortress of Chitor. This is the famous *Jaya Stambha*, "Pillar of Victory," which still stands erect in Chitor, and which the people more generally call *Kirtti Kambh*, or "Pillar of Fame."

During his long reign of fifty years Râna Kumbho built the strong fortress of *Kumbhalmer* to command a pass in the Aravalli range, leading from Udaypur to Jodhpur. It is 50 miles nearly north from Udaypur, 100 miles nearly south from Jodhpur, and the same distance west from Chitor. It was reconnoitred by Mahmud from a neighbouring hill. He wished to besiege it, but was obliged to give up his wish with the acknowledgment that the siege would be too long. Kumbho was at last murdered by his eldest son *Oda*, in A.D. 1468; but the murderer did not enjoy the throne long, as he was supplanted five years later by *Raimal* or *Ranmal*, the father of the famous *Sangrâma*.

Râna Sangrâma, or *Râna Sanga*, as he is most commonly called by the people, succeeded in A.D. 1508. He is styled by Tod the *Kalas*, or "Pinnacle," of Mewâr glory, because he fought with the Emperor Baber a very severe

---

[57] Briggs, iv. p. 224.

battle at *Kânwa.* I have visited the place, which the people believe to be haunted at midnight by long processions of the ghosts of the slain.

Sangrama's coins are square pieces of copper of the Muhammadan kings of Malwa, restruck on one face only with the Râna's name and the date of the Samvat year; while the other side still retains the name and titles of the Muhammadan king, either complete or in part. On one piece the obverse only gives the name of Sangrâma with the Hindu date, the rest of the type being the remains of the Muhammadan inscription.

The remaining coins of the Mewâr princes, Vikramâditya and Banbir, are even ruder than those of Sangrâma. I have given one specimen of each in Plate X.

As the Mewâr coinage begins with that of Râna Kumbho it is not necessary to give a long list of the kings. I therefore commence the following list with Râna Mokalji, the father of Kumbho, and conclude it with Râna Udaya, during whose reign Chitor was successfully besieged by Akbar in A.D. 1580.

GOBHILA RÂNAS OF MEWÂR.

Accession.		RANAS.	
Sam.	A.D.		
1454	1397	Mokalji	
1475	1418	Kumbhakarṇa	Kumbho
1525	1468	Oda	
1530	1473	Raimal, or Ranmal	
1565	1508	Sangrâma	Sanga
1586	1529	Ratna	
1589	1532	Vikramâditya	
1596	1539	Baṇbir	
1597	1540	Udaya Singha	

The only known money of the Rânas of Mewâr is of copper, and square in form, after the old Hindu fashion. The earliest specimens are those of Râna Kumbho, "*coined in his own name*," which were so unceremoniously refused by the Muhammadan king. These copper pieces are called *tankas* in the histories, which was the common Hindu name for the copper *Kârshapana*, which had been adopted, as well as the square form, by the Muhammadan kings of Malwa and the neighbouring states. Thus I find that

1. Muhammad Khan of Bayâna presented *tankas* to Mahmud.—Briggs, iv., p. 215.
2. Mahmud received 1¼ lakh of *tankas* from Kota-Bundi.—Briggs, iv., p. 215.
3. Mahmud received 16 lakhs of tankas from Rai of Champaner.—Briggs, iv., p. 215.

COPPER COINS OF THE RÂNAS OF MEWÂR.

PLATE X. No.	Grs.	RÂNA KUMBHAKARṆA, OF KUMBHO, A.D. 1418—1468.
11	196	Author, from Nimach. *Obv.*—Four lines of Nâgari inscription, with a small square in middle. *Sri Ekalingasya Prasâdât*, S. 151* (unit figure lost), centre illegible. *Rev.*—Four lines of Nâgari inscription. *Sri Kumbha**. * * * * *Rânâ* * A. *Ma * si sya.*
12	32	Author, from Stacy's collection. (See Prinsep, by E. Thomas, xxiv. 26.) *Obv.*—*Ekalinga.* *Rev.*—*Kumbhakarna.* *Ekalinga* is a famous temple a few miles to the north of Udaypur.

PLATE X.

RÂNÂ SANGRÂMA = A.D. 1508—1529.

No.	Grs.			
13	127	Author. *Obv.*—Four lines Nâgari letters.	*Sri* *Sangrâma* *Sâha, fi ?* 157*	*Rev.*—Jumble of Arabic legend of Malwa coin of Mahmud II.
14	59	Author. *Obv.*—Three lines Nâgari letters.	*Sri* *Sangrâma* *Sâha*, 1581 (A.D. 1524).	*Rev.*—Remains of Arabic legend of Mahmud II. of Malwa.
15		Author. *Obv.*—Top line Nâgari= Two lower lines of Arabic legend upside down.	*Sri Raja Sa* *us Sultân* *bin us Sultân* 1576 (= A.D. 1519)	*Rev.*—Two lines of Arabic legend *Mahmud Shah al Khalji ibn Nusrat Shah.*

RÂNA VIKRAMÂDITYA, A.D. 1532.

No.	Grs.			
16	188	Author; five specimens. *Obv.*—Three lines of Nâgari	[*Ra*] *ṇa Sri* *Vikramâdi-* [*tya*] 159* (=A.D. 1533).	*Rev.*—Remains of Arabic legend of Mahmud II. of Malwa.

RÂṆA BAṆBIR, A.D. 1539.

No.	Grs.			
17	125	Author; four specimens. *Obv.*— Top line illegible.	[*Sri*] *Baṇbîr* S. 159* (=A.D. 1539).	*Rev.*—Remains of Arabic legend of Mahmud II. of Malwa.

MODERN COINS OF MEWAR.

No.	Grs.				
18	167	Author; one rupee. *Obv.*—Mountain with three peaks. Nâgari legend in two lines	*Chitrakuta* *Udayapura*	*Rev.*—In an eight-sided scallop Nâgari	*Dosti* *Landhan*
—	41	Author; small coin, ¼ rupee.			

I obtained the first coin of this curious money in

PLATE XI.

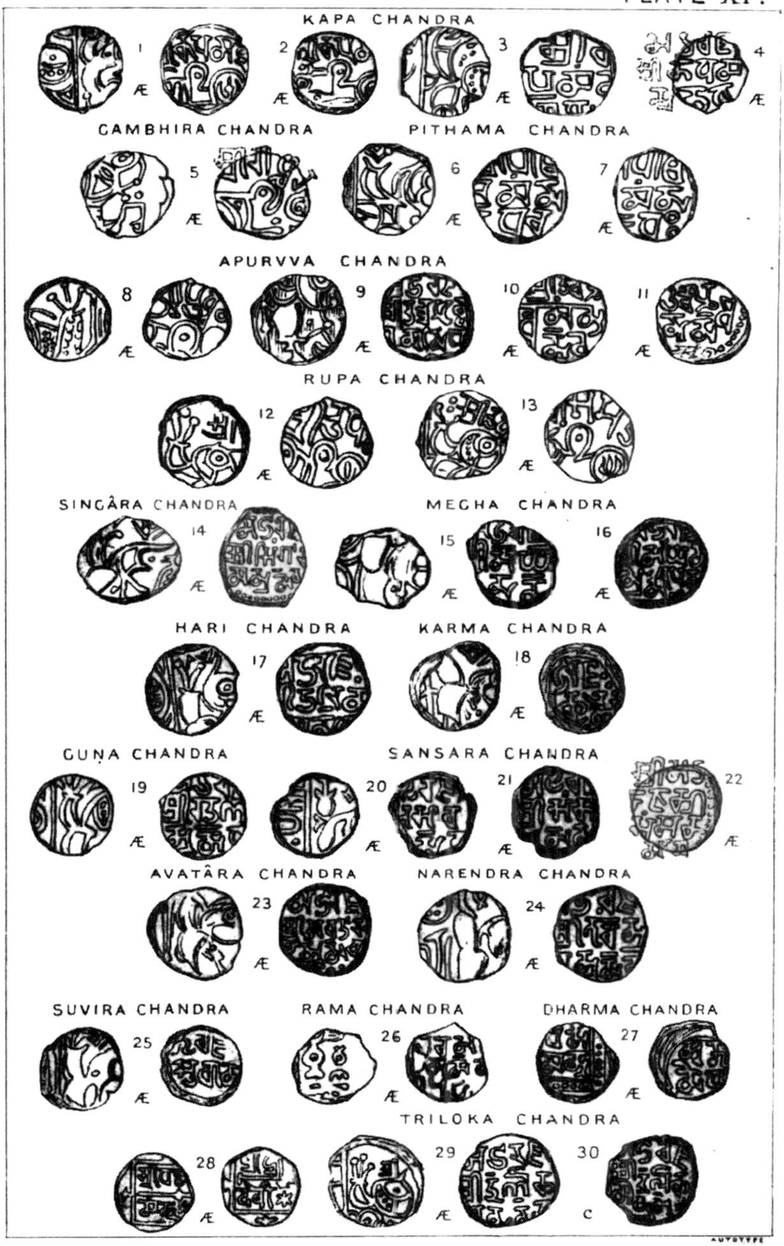

TRIGARTTA OR KANGRA.

PLATE X. No.	Grs.	
		1856 in Lahor before the mutiny. I have since seen a gold mohur of the same type. *Chitrakuta*, or *Chitor*, is the famous fortress of Mewar, and *Udayapur* is the present capital. The legend, *Friend of London*, was used before the mutiny.

INDOR.

JESWANT RAO HOLKAR.

No.	Grs.	
19	178	Author; duplicate, Prinsep's *Useful Tables*, p. 60; rupee. The following description is from Prinsep. His coin weighed 174·95 grains and its pure contents 165·84 grains. *Obv.*—*Srî Indraprasthasthito râjâ chakravartî bhûmaṇdale,* *Tatprasâdât kritâ mudrâ lokesmin vai virâjite,* *Rev.*—*Lakshmîkântapadâmbhojabhramararâjitachetasaḥ,* *Yeṣawantasya vikhyâtâ mudraisha prithivîtale.* "By permission of the King of Indraprastha [Delhi], the Emperor of the World, this coin has been struck by the renowned Yeswant, whose heart is as the black bee of the lotus foot of Lakshmikant, to circulate throughout the earth. Saka, 1728" [=A.D. 1806].

XI.—TRIGARTTA, OR JALANDHAR, OR KANGRA.

The rich district of Jalandhar originally comprised the two Doâbs lying between the rivers Râvi and Satlej. The capital of the country was the city of *Jalandhar*, and *Kot-Kangra* was its chief stronghold. The name was derived from the Danava Jalandhara, the son of the Ocean and the Ganges River. The legend about his defeat by Siva I have related in another place.[57] The full name of the

[57] *Archæol. Survey of India*, v. 146.

province was *Jalandhar-pith*, or "Jalandhar's back," as the Titan was said to have laid prostrate on his back after his defeat. This name was only slightly altered by Akbar to *Jalandhar-Bit* (or *Bist*). The Titan's mouth is said to be at *Jwala-mukhi* or the "Flaming mouth," and his feet at Multân.

Another name for the country lying between the Râvi and Satlej is *Trigartta*, or "Watered by Three Rivers," the Râvi, the Byâs, and the Satlej. This is the classical name which Hema Chandra uses when he says *Jalandharâs Trigartâḥ syuḥ*, or "Jalandhara, *i.e.* Trigarta." This is the common name still in use, which has been handed down from the time of the Mahâbhârata and the Purânas.

The royal family of Traigarta derived their descent from Susarmah Chandra of Multân, who fought in the Great War against the Pândavas. After the war they retired to the hills, where they built the fort of Kangra. As Chandravansis they all bore the name of Chandra, which they have kept until the present day. The inscription in the temple of Baijnâth, at Kiragrâma, which is dated in A.D. 804, names *Jaya Chandra* as the Raja of Jalandhar;[58] and towards the end of the same century Kalhana Pandit records that *Prithvi Chandra*, Raja of Trigartta, fled before the army of Sankara Varma. His son was *Bhuvana Chandra*. At a later date, about A.D. 1040, Kalhana mentions *Indu Chandra* as the Raja of Jalandhara.[59] The same cognomen is found upon all their coins as shown in Plate XI.

The famous fort of *Kângra*, called commonly *Kôt*-

---

[58] *Archæol. Survey of India*, v. 181.
[59] *Raja Tarangini*, v. 144, 145; vii. 150, 182.

Kangra, occupies a strong position on the precipitous fork of the hill at the junction of the Mânjhi and Bân-Gangâ Rivers. There is no notice of the place before the time of Mahmûd in A.D. 1009. Its walls are upwards of two miles in circuit, but its strength does not lie in its works, but in its precipitous cliffs, which on the side of the Bân-Gangâ rise to a height of 300 feet. It has often been captured since Mahmud took it, but the Rajas still continued to reign as tributaries of its captors.

Our first detailed notice of the Rajas of Kangra is in the reign of *Rûpa Chandra,* in the time of Feroz Taghlak, A.D. 1360—1370. The Raja made a timely submission as related by his own descendant, Raja Mânikya Chandra, as well as by the Muhammadan historians, Shams-i-Sirâj and Ferishta.

Raja Sansâra Chandra I. was a tributary of the Delhi King, Muhammad Sayid, in A.D. 1433—1446 ; but the fort must have fallen into the hands of the native rulers, as Sher-Shah, about A.D. 1520, sent his famous general Khawâs against it, when it was captured once more.

Whenever a favourable opportunity seemed to offer itself, the Rajas usually rebelled, and were always soon after reduced. The reputed strength of the fort suggested rebellion and Kangra was successively taken by Akbar, by Jahângir, and by Aurangzeb. It was very secure against bows and arrows, but was unsafe against matchlocks, as the whole of the interior was overlooked from a neighbouring hill.

COINS OF THE KANGRA RAJAS.

The coins current at Kangra in early times must have been the copper money of the Indo-Scythian Kushâns and the silver money of the Indo-Greek Princes Menander and Apollodotus. In fact, a large number of the silver pieces of Apollodotus were found in a field at *Jwâla mukhi.* This money apparently remained in use until the mediæval period of the Brahman Kings of Kabul, whose coins, and more especially those of *Sâmanta Deva,* were issued in such numbers that no new coinage was attempted by succeeding princes, and they remained until the Muhammadan conquest almost the sole currency of the Panjab and North-West India. The Ghazni Kings of Lahor, Masäud, Modûd, Ibrahim and Farokhzâd, and the Hindu kings of North-West India, the Tomars Sallakshan Pâl and Anang Pâl, the Rahtor Madan Pâl, and the Chauhân Prithvi Raja, all adopted the type of the horseman with the title of Sri Sâmanta Deva.

The coins shown in Plate XI. were all drawn by my own hand upwards of forty years ago, and more than thirty years ago the plate was sent to Calcutta for publication in the Journal of the Bengal Asiatic Society. But it was afterwards returned to me as there was some difficulty about getting it engraved in Calcutta. Since then the whole of my collection of Kângra coins has been lost in the wreck of the steamer *Indus,* off Ceylon. It included many good specimens of the known Rajas, acquired since 1850, besides an unique specimen of the royal poet Mânikya Chandra Deva.

In 1853 Sir Clive Bayley published a short notice of the coins of the Kangra Rajas, including the money of eight kings. He refers to my previous notice of "*some years before*" (see *Prinsep's Antiquities,* by E. Thomas, i., 392) in which I had made known the names of fourteen kings. I notice this paper of Sir Clive Bayley because he states his opinion that these coins are "evidently descended from the Bull and Horseman type." They are, he goes on to say, " coarsely executed imitations " of them, with the common superscription of " *Sri Sâmanta Deva.*"

This also was my opinion when I arranged Plate XI. in 1850. Mr. C. J. Rodgers came to the same conclusion. He says, " all the coins of the Kângra Râjas, with some few rare exceptions, are of the Horseman type. Some are of the Bull and Horseman type, with the names of the Râjas over the Bulls. Nay, more than this, the earliest Kângra coins bear the name of Sâmanta Deva over the Bull." This is the very same conclusion that Bayley and myself had arrived at more than forty years ago. The earliest coins of the Kângra mint bear the name of *Sri Sâmanta Deva.* The next step was to place the name of the Kangra Raja over the Bull, as in Nos. 1 and 2 of *Kapa* Chandra, No. 5 of *Gambhîra Chandra,* and No. 12 of *Rupa Chandra.* But No. 13 of Rupa Chandra gives the Raja's name over the Horseman, and that of Sâmanta Deva over the Bull.

I have given a coin of *Guṇa Chandra* of Guler because he was the son of *Hari*-Chandra, A.D. 1405 to 1420. There is a curious story attached to the foundation of the *Guler Râj* by Hari Chandra.[60] He and Karmma Chandra were brothers, and Hari, as the elder brother, succeeded his father as Raja of *Trigartta.* Some years after his accession he fell down a well at Harsar when out sporting, and could not be found. His younger brother, Karmma, was then proclaimed Raja, and his wives became Satis. After a few days he was discovered by a *Baipâri,* who got him out of the well and revived him. But as his funeral ceremonies had been performed he could not recover his

[60] *Archæol. Survey of India,* v. 151.

original kingdom and was obliged to be content with a portion of Guler. As a reward to the Baipâri for his assistance, Hari Chandra remitted all duties on his goods, an exception which was respected by the succeeding Rajas, including the Sikhs, and only became obsolete on the general remission of all duties by the British Government.

Rajas of Trigartta or Kangra.

Accession.		According to Lists.	Coins.
Sam.	A.D.		
		Jaya Chandra	
		Prithivi Chandra	
		Bhuvana Chandra	
		Indu Chandra	
	1315	Jaya Sinha Chandra	
	1330	Prithvi Chandra	Pithama Chandra D.
	1345	Purva Chandra	Apurvva Chandra D.
	1360	Rûpa Chandra	Rûpa Chandra D.
	1375	Sringâra Chandra	Singâra Chandra D.
1447	1390	Megha Chandra	Megha Chandra D.
1462	1405	Hari Chandra	Hari Chandra D.
		Guṇa Chandra	[Raja of Guler]
1457	1420	Karma Chandra	Karmma Chandra D.
1492	1435	Sansâra Chandra	Sansâra Chandra D.
1507	1450	Devânga Chandra	Avatâra Chandra D.
1522	1465	Narendra Chandra	Narendra Chandra D.
1537	1480	Suvîra Chandra	Suvîra Chandra D.
1552	1495	Prayâga Chandra	
1567	1510	Râma Chandra	Râma Chandra D.
1585	1528	Dharma Chandra	Dharma Chandra D.
1620	1563	Mânikya Chandra	Manikya Chandra D.
1627	1570	Jaya Chandra	
1642	1585	Vriddhi Chandra	
1667	1610	Triloka Chandra	Triloka Chandra D.

Copper Coins of Rajas of Kangra.

Plate XI. No.	Date.	Obverse.	Reverse.
	A.D.		
		KAPA-CHANDRA.	
1		Horseman . .	Recumbent Bull *Sri Kapa Chandra*
2		Do. . .	
3		Do. . .	Recumbent Bull *Sri Kapa Chandra*
4		Do. . .	
		GAMBHIRA CHANDRA.	
5		Horseman . .	Recumbent Bull *Sri Gambhira Chandra*
	1330	**PITHAMA CHANDRA = PRITHVI. CH.**	
6		Horseman . .	Recumbent Bull *Sri Pithama Chandra*
7		Do. . .	
	1345	**APURVVA CHANDRA.**	
8		Horseman . .	Recumbent Bull *Sri Apurvva Chandra*
9		Horseman . .	*Maharaja Sri* *Apurvva Chandra Deva*
10		Do. . .	
11		Do. . .	
	1360	**RUPA CHANDRA.**	
12		Horseman. Sri .	Recumbent Bull *Sri Rupa Chandra Deva*
13		Horseman . . *Sri Rupa* [*Chandra*]	Recumbent Bull *Sri Sâmanta*
	1375	**SINGARA CHANDRA.**	
14		Horseman. *Sri* .	*Maharaja Sri* *Singàra Chandra Deva*

Copper Coins of Rajas of Kangra—*continued.*

PLATE XI. No.	Date.	Obverse.	Reverse.
	A.D.		
	1390	MEGHA CHANDRA.	
15		Horseman . .	*Mahárája Sri*
16		Do. . .	*Megha Chandra Deva*
	1405	HARI-CHANDRA.	
17		Horseman . .	*Mahârâja Sri Hari-Chandra Deva*
	1420	KARMA CHANDRA.	
18		Horseman . .	*Mahârâja Sri Karmma Chandra Deva*
	1420	GUṆA-CHANDRA.	
19		Horseman . .	*Mahárája Sri Guṇa Chandra Deva*
	1435	SANSÂRA-CHANDRA.	
20		Horseman . .	*Mahárája Sri*
21		Do. . .	*Sansára Chandra*
22		Do. . .	*Deva*

N.B.—Guṇa Chandra was the son of Hari Chandra, and succeeded his father as Raja of *Guler*, of which Haripur was the capital. The story of Hari Chandra's accession to the *gadi* of Guler has been told in a previous page. The coins of Hari Chandra are common, and I conclude that some of them were struck as Raja of Kangra, and some as Raja of Guler. There are no coins of his successors except this one of his son, Guṇa Chandra.

Copper Coins of Rajas of Kangra—*continued.*

PLATE XI. No.	Date.	Obverse.	Reverse.
	A.D.		
	1450	AVATÂRA-CHANDRA.	
23		Horseman . .	*Maharaja Sri Avatâra Chandra Deva*
		N.B.—The name of *Avatâra* does not occur in any of the lists of the Rajas of Kangra, but I believe that it is only a synonym for *Devânga*, of whom I formerly possessed one coin kindly given to me by Mr. C. J. Rodgers.	
	1465	NARENDRA CHANDRA.	
24		Horseman . .	*Mahârâja Sri Narendra Chandra Deva*
	1480	SUVÎRA CHANDRA.	
25		Horseman . .	*Mahârâja Sri Narendra Chandra Deva*
	1510	RÂMA-CHANDRA.	
26		Unknown symbols .	[*Mahârâja*] *Sri Râma Chandra Deva* s. 1585 = A.D. 1528
		N.B.—This is the only specimen of a dated coin that I have met with.	
	1528	DHARMA-CHANDRA.	
27		*Dharma Chandra* .	*Mungga Deva* (?)
28		*Sri Dharma Chandra*	* *dra Devi*

COPPER COINS OF RAJAS OF KANGRA—*continued.*

PLATE XI. No.	PLATE XI. Date.	Obverse.	Reverse.
	A.D.		
	1563	MANIKYA-CHANDRA.	
—		* * * *	*Mahârâja Sri* *Manikya Chandra Deva*
		N.B.—This unique coin was lost with all my Kangra collection in the wreck of the Indus steamer. It was a large thick piece, with the legend in Nâgari letters.	
	1610	TRILOKA-CHANDRA.	
29		Horseman. *Sri* .	*Mahârâja Sri* *Triloka Chandra Deva*
30		Horseman . .	Same legend as No. 29